Baseball's Great Dynasties
THE
CUBS

Baseball's Great Dynasties

THE

Thomas G. Aylesworth

GALLERY BOOKS
An imprint of W.H. Smith Publishers Inc.
112 Madison Avenue
New York, New York 10016

Published by Gallery Books
A Division of W H Smith Publishers Inc.
112 Madison Avenue
New York, New York 10016

Produced by
Brompton Books Corp.
15 Sherwood Place
Greenwich, CT 06830

ISBN 0-8317-0657-0

Printed in Hong Kong

10 9 8 7 6 5 4 3 2 1

PICTURE CREDITS

The Bettmann Archive: 1, 4-5, 11, 15(top), 24, 30-31(bottom), 75(top left).
Brompton Photo Library: 8, 9(top left), 17, 39(right), 75(bottom right).
Chevrolet Motor Division, General Motors Corp: 30(top left).
Courtesy, Chicago Cubs, photo by Stephen Green: 76-77.
Malcolm Emmons: 7(bottom), 47, 49, 50(top left), 52(bottom left), 54, 60.
Nancy Hogue: 52(top right), 56, 57, 58-59.
Ron Modra: 70-71.
National Baseball Library, Cooperstown, NY: 6(left), 10, 12, 13(both), 14, 15(bottom), 16, 18(right), 19(both), 20(both), 21(both), 22(both), 23, 25(top left), 26(top), 27(bottom), 28(bottom), 30(top right), 33(top), 34, 35, 36(both), 44, 45, 67(top).
Ponzini Photography: 2, 3, 6(right), 7(top both), 61, 62, 63(both), 64, 65(all three), 66, 67(bottom both), 68(both), 69, 70, 73(all four).
Topps Baseball Cards: 51(all three).
UPI/Bettmann Newsphotos: 8-9(bottom), 9(top right), 18(left), 25(bottom right), 26(bottom), 27(top), 28(top), 29, 32, 33(bottom), 37(both), 38, 39(left), 40(both), 41, 42, 43, 46, 48, 50(bottom right), 53, 54, 72, 74.
Endpaper photo courtesy of Chicago Cubs.

ACKNOWLEDGMENTS

The author and publisher would like to thank the following people who have helped in the preparation of this book: Sydney L. Mayer, who edited it; Don Longabucco, who designed it; Rita Longabucco, who did the picture research; and Cynthia Klein, who prepared the index.

Page 1: *"The Peerless Leader" Frank Chance at bat. In the 15 years that the speedy first baseman played for the Cubs, from 1898 to 1912, they went to the World Series four times. Chance, who stole 10 bases in Series play, was elected to the Hall of Fame in 1946.*

Page 2: *Andre Dawson at bat against the Mets. Dawson joined the Cubs in 1987, and promptly turned in an MVP season.*

Page 3: *The Cubs' first baseman Mark Grace batted .314 during the 1989 season, and .647 during the NLCS.*

This page: *A platoon of catchers poses during Spring Training in 1937. From left to right: Robert Garbark, James O'Dea, Charles "Gabby" Hartnett and Harold Sueme.*

Contents

Preface 6

1. Origins 10

2. The Beginning of Modern Times 16

3. A Dynasty Begins 24

4. The Dynasty Ends 34

5. Times of Struggle 46

6. On the Move Again 60

7. Odds and Ends 74

Cub Achievements 78

Index 80

Preface

It seems I was always destined to be a Cubs fan, and it all started in 1933, when my parents moved to Chicago and settled into an apartment just four blocks from Wrigley Field. During the spring and early autumn I could hear the cheers of the fans through the open windows of my elementary school. Those were glory years, and we kids had heroes aplenty – future Hall of Famers Billy Herman, Gabby Hartnett,

Kiki Cuyler, Dizzy Dean, Chuck Klein, Freddie Lindstrom and Burleigh Grimes.

This was the period when the Cubs somehow contrived to win the pennant every three years, just like clockwork – 1929, 1932, 1935, 1938. And these were also the years when we learned to hate the Yankees, who wiped out the Cubs by sweeping the 1932 and 1938 World Series. I became the only North Sider who never claimed to be at the ball park in 1938 when player-manager Gabby Harnett hit his "Homer in the Gloamin'," although I insist I was listening to the game on radio.

It seemed that the winning would go on forever, but that was not to be. Still, win or lose, I remained loyal. For two summers I took courses in Lewis Towers of Loyola University on the Near North Side, and if I could finish my assigned reading by the time the El train reached Addison Street,

and the Cubs were at home, I usually rewarded myself with a trip to Wrigley Field. I saw a lot of ball games that way, and I marveled at the likes of Eddie Waitkus, Peanuts Lowrey, Bill Nicholson, Andy Pafko, Phil Cavarretta, Bob Scheffing, Stan Hack, Hank Borowy, Johnny Schmitz,

Above left: *Ryne Sandberg won the Most Valuable Player Award in 1984 when the Cubs won the Eastern Division Title.*

Above: *Rick Sutcliffe won the Cy Young Award in 1984, the first Cub to do so in decades.*

Left: *Glenn Beckert was the Cubs' star second baseman during the 1960s. His excellent record was surpassed only by Sandberg's in the 1980s.*

Claude Passeau, Bob Rush and the immortal Emil Verban.

After winning their pennant in 1945 it took 39 years for the Cubs to take another one – they were National League East champions in 1984. But even with all those years of frustration, the team still gave their fans excitement. Sometimes this excitement consisted of rage at some of the trades they made. Why, oh why, did they trade aways such superstars as Lou Brock, Ferguson Jenkins, Rick Reuschel, Bruce Sutter, Bill Madlock, Jose Cardinal, Bill Buckner, Rafael Palmeiro, Keith Moreland and Jody Davis? For that matter, why, oh why did they want Dave Kingman on the team?

Still, there were other kinds of excitement provided by the many superstars who played for the Cubs from the 1950s on. There were future Hall of Famers Ernie Banks, Billy Williams, Monte Irvin, Ralph Kiner, Robin Roberts and Hoyt Wilhelm. There were men elected by the fans to the All-Star team, men such as Hank Sauer (twice), Ron Santo (four times), Don Kessinger (four times), Glenn Beckert (twice), Dave Kingman (once), Ryne Sandberg (five times) and Andre Dawson (twice), plus many other Cubs who appeared in the games. There were also National League Most Valuable Players Dawson, Sandberg, Banks (twice) and Sauer. There were Cy Young Award winners Ferguson Jenkins, Bruce Sutter and Rick Sutcliffe, plus Rookies of the Year Billy Williams and Ken Hubbs.

And we Cub fans can still find consolation of a sort in the wonderful play *Bleacher Bums*. First presented in 1977 and revived in 1989, the play features actors sitting in the bleachers of Wrigley Field and commenting on the game between the Cardinals and the Cubs. It does glorify the Chicagoans, and every night the Cubs are ahead by three runs in the ninth inning. But every night a Cardinal player hits a grand slam home run to win the game. Designed for Cub fans who have become slightly paranoid (and most of us have), it still has the ring of truth. For, to paraphrase the novelist James Michener (who was writing about the Philadelphia Phillies), "Young man, when you root for the Cubs, you acquire a sense of tragedy."

Right: *"Handsome Ransom Jackson" was the Cubs' third baseman in the early 1950s. Unfortunately his hitting and fielding did not match his looks.*

Far right: *The 1950s were not all bleak for the Cubs. Ernie Banks, seen here batting in front of a sparse New York crowd, won the Most Valuable Player Award in 1958 and 1959. He is the only Cub and the only National Leaguer ever to have won this award in consecutive years.*

Above left: *The Cubs' infield during 1950 spring training on Catalina Island. From left to right: shortstop Roy Smalley Sr., third baseman Bill Serena, second baseman Wayne Terwilliger and first baseman Preston Ward. This infield formed the famous Terwilliger to Smalley to grandstand double-play combination.*

Above: *The legendary Emil Verban, the Stalwart, second baseman for the Cubs in the late 1940s. His bravery and endurance under fire of enemy hitters brought him immortality when the Emil Verban Society was formed a few years ago, honoring both him and the characteristics he displayed. Among the Society's most prominent members are Ronald Reagan, George Will and Tom Bosley. The society meets once a year but no longer in the White House.*

1. Origins

When the first professional baseball league was established the team that was to become the Cubs was there. It happened in Collier's Cafe on Broadway and 13th Street in New York on March 17, 1871. Ten men were present when the National Association of Base-Ball Players was founded, and nine of them put up $10 for a franchise in the new circuit. Charter members were the Chicago White Stockings (later the Cubs), the Philadelphia Athletics, the Boston Red Stockings, the Cleveland Forest Citys, the New York Mutuals, the Rockford (Illinois) Forest

William A. Hulbert helped form the National League in 1876, of which the Chicago White Stockings (later the Cubs) were charter members.

Citys, the Washington Nationals, the Washington Olympics and the Fort Wayne (Indiana) Kekiogas. The Fort Wayne team withdrew in August and was replaced by the Brooklyn Eckfords.

It wasn't a strong league. Players would jump from team to team, some teams played many more games than others and gambling and drunkenness were endemic. It was the owner of the White Stockings who decided to correct the situation. William Ambrose Hulbert called a secret meeting in Louisville, Kentucky, in January, 1876, to convince representatives of the teams from St. Louis, Cincinnati and Louisville to join the Chicago club in a new league – the National League of Professional Base Ball Clubs. They agreed, and Hulbert was off to New York, where he held a meeting in the Grand Central Hotel with representatives of the Boston, Hartford, Philadelphia and New York clubs. Thus the National League was born in the same year that General George Armstrong Custer suffered his defeat at the Little Big Horn. It is said that Hulbert locked the door to the hotel room as he read the proposed constitution that he and his right-hand man, superstar pitcher Al Spalding, had prepared.

The rules were strict. Gambling and alcohol were forbidden in the stadiums, every franchise had to be located in a city with at least 75,000 people, each team had to pay annual dues of $100 and play 70 games – ten with every other club (five at home and five away). Admission to the games was to be 50 cents (quite a high price for the time), and the team that won the most games would get a pennant costing no less than $100.

Players were bound to their club through a reserve clause and could no longer jump from team to team. Morgan P. Bulkeley, the owner of the Hartford Blues (a team that was later to move to Brooklyn), was chosen as president of a five-man committee that would control the new organization.

During the first year, 1876, New York and Philadelphia refused to make their

An 1877 portrait of the first National League champions of 1876, led by pitcher-manager A.G. Spalding. The Cubs were to win 16 National League pennants between 1876 and 1945.

final western trip, and Hulbert, who had replaced Bulkeley as president, astonished everyone by expelling the two clubs from the league. Boston and Chicago were the only charter member teams still in the league at the start of the 1878 season, but Cincinnati paid up its back dues, and other teams from Providence, Indianapolis and Milwaukee rounded out the league of six teams.

Many franchises were shifted during the first 25 years of the National League, with only Boston and Chicago remaining unchanged as charter members. Teams from 23 cities came in and went out of the league, including St. Louis, Hartford, Louisville, New York, Philadelphia, Cincinnati, Providence, Indianapolis, Milwaukee, Buffalo, Cleveland, Syracuse, Troy, Worcester, Detroit, Kansas City, Washington, DC, Brooklyn, Pittsburgh and Baltimore. In 1900 the league settled down into the same eight franchises it would maintain for the next 53 years: Chicago, Pittsburgh, Philadelphia, Brooklyn, St. Louis, Boston, New York and Cincinnati.

Managed by future Hall of Famer Al Spalding (who went on to found the sporting goods company), the White Stockings ran away with the league's first pennant in 1876, finishing six games ahead of St. Louis. Not only was Spalding the manager, he was also the star pitcher for the team, winning 47 of the 52 games on the schedule. The league's first batting champion was Chicago second baseman Ross Barnes, who

Cap Anson was both first baseman and manager of the Chicago White Stockings from 1879 to 1897, leading them to the pennant in 1880, 1881, 1882, 1885 and 1886.

versity of Notre Dame in 1869, where he had organized the school's first baseball team, being its captain and third baseman. As a major league first baseman, Anson was the first player to get 3000 hits, the first to get three consecutive home runs in a game and the first to complete two unassisted double plays in a game. It was said that he was so quick that he was never hit by a pitched ball – quite an accomplishment in those rough and ready days. When he closed out his 22-year career with the White Stockings in 1897 he hit two home runs in a game with St. Louis on October 3, making him, at age 46, the oldest man ever to hit a major-league roundtripper.

As a manager, he was a strict disciplinarian, as well as being quite an innovator. He forbade his players to drink, smoke or use drugs. He introduced the hit-and-run play and was the first manager to use hand signals. Anson also popularized base stealing and pitching rotations.

In 1880 the White Stockings came in first again (67-17), 15 games ahead of Providence, and Anson continued his brilliant leadership in 1881, winning yet another pennant by finishing 56-28 – ten games ahead of Providence. There were two highlights during that season. Chicago centerfielder George "Piano Legs" Gore stole a record seven bases in one game on June 25, and the White Stockings were involved in setting another record in Troy, New York: on the last day of the season Chicago was playing the fifth-place Haymakers in a torrential downpour, and the game was witnessed by just 12 die-hard Haymaker fans – a mark that still stands as the fewest ever to watch a major-league baseball game. It was also in that year the Chicago pitcher Larry Corcoran won 45 games and didn't even lead the league.

It was first place again in 1882 (55-29), as the White Stockings finished three games ahead of Providence. Just two pitchers combined that year to win all the games – Corcoran won 40 and Fred Goldsmith won 44. But it was second place (59-39) in 1883, when they ended up four games behind Boston. Corcoran had slipped to 34 wins and Goldsmith was at 25. The White Stockings did show some power in 1883, when they set a record for the most runs scored in one inning, 18.

Anson did have his darker side, however. Indeed, he may have been responsible for the unwritten rule against blacks playing in the major leagues, a rule that wasn't broken until Jackie Robinson broke the modern color barrier in 1947. At least 20 blacks had played major league ball on mostly white teams in the 1880s, but on May 1, 1884, Chicago was scheduled to play

hit .429 and also hit the league's first home run against Cincinnati on May 2.

Chicago fell to fifth place the next year, finishing with a 26-33 record, 15½ games out of first, and Spalding was gone. Under manager Bob Ferguson it was fourth place (30-30 and 11 games out) in 1878. First baseman and future Hall of Famer "Cap" Anson was named player-manager for the 1879 season and brought them in in fourth again (46-33 and 11½ games out).

Anson had been a student at the Uni-

an exhibition game with Toledo of the American Association (which was then considered to be a major league). On the Toledo team were two black brothers – Moses Fleetwood Walker and Welday Walker. When Anson saw Fleetwood Walker take the field, he shouted, "Get that nigger off the field." Chicago was forced to forfeit the game.

Then, in 1887, when the New York National League team tried to play another black man, George Stovey, Anson declared, "There's a law against that." Stovey, furious, left the game and never played again. That was what set the precedent, and black players were barred from major-league baseball for 50 years.

The White Stockings came in in fourth (62-50) in 1884, 22 games behind the first-place Providence club. That was the year that future Hall of Fame pitcher John Clarkson joined the club, although he won but ten games.

Clarkson came into his own in 1885 as he went 53-16 to lead the league in wins. It was another pennant year for the White Stockings, as they finished in first place (87-25), beating out New York by two games. It was also the year that Anson invented the idea of spring training. The White Stockings were the first team to head south in the spring when they went to Hot Springs, Arkansas. Actually, the purpose was not so much to prepare for the season in a warmer

climate as it was to dry out the team's off-season drunks.

It was another pennant (90-34) in 1886, when Chicago finished two and one-half games ahead of the Detroit Wolverines. Future Hall of Fame outfielder King Kelly led the league in hitting, with a .388 batting average. In 1887 the White Stockings stunned the baseball world by selling, at the end of the season, star pitcher Clarkson, who had gone 38-21, to Boston for $10,000 – an astronomical sum. But after all, he was a Harvard man. That year it was a third-place finish (71-50), but the team was only six and one-half games behind the first place St. Louis club.

The White Stockings climbed to second (77-58) in 1888, ten games behind New York. Anson himself led the league in batting that year, with a .344 average. Then it was third (67-65) in 1889, trailing first place New York by 19 games. In 1890 it was second place (84-53), six games behind Brooklyn. Right-handed pitcher Bill Hutchinson assumed Clarkson's mantle as he went 42-25 and led the league in wins. Center fielder Walt Wilmot also led the league, hitting an astonishing 14 home runs.

In 1891 it was second again (82-53), three and one-half games behind Boston, and Hutchinson (43-19) once again led the league in wins. In 1892 the White Stockings fell to seventh (70-76), 30 games behind the

Above left:
Outfielder Mike "King" Kelly led the league in hitting for the White Stockings in 1886.

Above: *Cap Anson was a snappy dresser and was much adored by Chicago ladies over 100 years ago.*

first-place Boston club in the 12-team league. Hutchinson had a so-so 37-34 record, but he did lead the league in wins again. It was ninth place (56-71) in 1893, 34 games behind Boston. The pitching staff had fallen apart, for Hutchinson went a dismal 16-23.

At the end of the 1893 season the club changed its name to the Chicago Colts. The name change didn't help much, as the Colts finished eighth (57-75) in 1894, trailing first-place Baltimore by 34 games. Only pitcher Clark Griffith (21-11) had a winning record. Perhaps the only interesting thing about that season was that Colts catcher Pop Schriver became the first man to catch a baseball dropped from the Washington Monument (from a height of 550 feet).

Anson finally turned the team around a bit in 1895, finishing fourth (72-58), only 15 games behind the first-place Baltimore Orioles. Then it was fifth (71-57) in 1896 – 18½ games back of the Baltimore team. In 1897 it was an awful ninth place (59-73), 34 games behind league-leading Boston. The only good thing that happened that year was that the club set a record by scoring 36 runs in a game against the Louisville Colonels on June 29, a record that still stands. At the end of the season Cap Anson was out, to be replaced by Tom Burns as manager, and the team changed its name

yet again – this time to the Chicago Orphans. Anson went to work as a vaudeville performer, then as a billiard- and bowling-hall proprieter and eventually as city clerk of Chicago.

In 1898 Burns brought the team in in fourth place (85-65), 17½ games behind the first-place Boston team. At the end of the season the Orphans finally became the Chicago Cubs. And then it was eighth place (75-73), trailing the Brooklyn club by 26½ games in 1899, and Burns was gone.

Nineteen hundred was the year in which the National League established a top salary limitation of $2400. The League also pared back to eight teams from 12.

Tom Loftus had come in to manage the Cubs and was able to skipper the Cubs to fifth place (65-75) in 1900, 17½ games behind the first-place Brooklyn team. In 1901 the Cubs finished sixth (53-86), 37 games behind the pennant-winning Pirates. That was enough for the front office, and Loftus was fired.

The next manager was Frank Selee, who brought the Cubs in in fifth place (68-69) in 1902, trailing the first-place Pirates by 37 games. Still, the club almost played .500 ball, and Selee was kept on. He would thus participate in an historical transition, for this was the end of old-time baseball. The modern era was about to begin.

Below: *The Chicago White Stockings in 1888. Anson is seated third from right.*

Above: *The Bloomington, Illinois Reds in 1887, where future Hall of Fame pitcher Clark Griffith, second from the left at the top, got his start. He was earning $65 a month that year. He went on to fame with the Colts (later the Cubs) and to fortune when he owned the American League Washington Senators.*

Left: *Frank Selee managed the Cubs at the turn of the century.*

2. The Beginning of Modern Times

Most sportspeople agree that the modern era of baseball began in 1903, since that was the year that the first World Series between the National and the two-year-old American League was played. That year Selee brought the Cubs in in a third place (82-56) finish, and they were only a game and a half out of second. In 1904 they moved up a notch to second (93-60), 13 games behind the Giants. With the presence of four future Hall of Famers on the team – pitcher Three Finger Brown, shortstop Joe Tinker, second baseman Johnny Evers and first baseman Frank Chance – a dynasty was building.

In 1905, with the team in fourth place (52-38), Selee left the club and the new manager was Frank Chance, who went 40-23, bringing them in in third (92-61). Then came the fateful year of 1906.

The Chicago Cubs in 1904, managed by Frank Selee, had Joe Tinker at shortstop, John Evers at second base and Frank Chance at first base.

In that year the Cubs won 116 games and lost only 36, a record that still stands. Much of their success was due to a pitching staff that included Three Finger Brown (26-6), Orval Overall (12-3), Ed Reulbach (19-4), Jack Taylor (12-3) and Carl Lundgren (17-6): they combined for a record 32 shutouts that year. It was a powerhouse team that scored 11 runs in the first inning off the Giants' aces Christy Mathewson and Joe McGinnity on June 7, winning the game 19-0. Pitcher Taylor finally was knocked out of the box by Brooklyn on August 13, after running up a string of 187 complete games and 15 relief games that he had finished without further relief help.

But the star of the show was Mordecai "Three Finger" "Miner" Brown. As a child in Nyesville, Indiana, he had mangled his right hand – his pitching hand – in a corn chopper. He had only an inch left of his index finger and his middle finger was grotesquely bent out of shape. This may actually have made his curve ball break more sharply. At any rate, he ended his 14-year career in 1916 with an earned run average of 2.06, the second best in baseball history, and a career strikeout total of 1375.

The Cubs won the pennant by 20 games over the Giants, and were heavy favorites to take the 1906 World Series against the White Sox in the first Fall Classic ever played between teams from the same city. After all, the Sox, called the "Hitless Wonders," had a team batting average of only .230 (the lowest in the American League),

with no team member batting as high as .280. The only reason they had won the American League pennant was that they had had an amazing 19-game winning streak in August.

White Sox pitcher Nick Altrock (20-13) beat Brown (26-6) in the opener 2-1, with each team getting but four hits. Then the Cubs' Ed Reulbach (19-4) helped the team even the Series with a one-hit 7-1 win over Doc White (18-6). The Sox' Ed Walsh (17-13) threw a two-hitter at Jack Pfiester (20-8) to win the third game 3-0. The Cubs came back in the fourth game when Brown had his own two-hitter and beat Altrock 1-0. But they had shot their wad. The Sox took the fifth game 8-6 (Walsh beating Pfiester), and the sixth game 8-3, (White beating Brown). The miracle had happened, and the Sox took the Series four games to two.

The Cubs roared back in 1907, once again on the strength of their pitching staff, which had a combined earned run average of 1.73, still the lowest in National League history. After winning the pennant (107-45), 17 games ahead of the Pirates, not to be denied, they went on to beat the Tigers in the World Series, four games to none, with one tie, making the Tigers the first team in history to be shut out in the World Series.

The first game ended in a 3-3 tie, being called on account of darkness. Orval Overall (23-8) of the Cubs faced Bill Donovan (25-4) in that game, and Donovan had a bit of misfortune when catcher Charlie Schmidt failed to hold a third strike in the

The pennant-winning Cubs in 1906 lost the World Series to the Chicago White Sox in the only City Series which ever coincided with the World Series. The City Series was played after the season almost every year until World War II broke out. And, it was often more important to Chicago fans than the World Series itself.

Above: *Mr. and Mrs. Franklin P. Adams on their way to Europe. Adams wrote the famous poem immortalizing "Tinker to Evers to Chance."*

Above right: *Fred Merkle, New York Giants first baseman whose "boner" helped the Cubs win the 1908 pennant.*

ninth inning, which cost the Tigers a 3-2 victory. The play generated some suspicion, because the Tiger player representative, Herman "Germany" Schaefer, had asked the baseball commission in a pre-Series meeting what its policy would be on sharing gate receipts if one of the first four games ended in a tie. The commission deliberated and decided that in the event of a tie, the players would have a share in the first five games, rather than the first four. So many cynics wondered if the game had been fixed. In an investigation, no skullduggery was found.

In any case, the Cubs won the second game 3-1 behind Pfiester (15-9), who beat George Mullin (20-20). Reulbach (17-4) beat Ed Siever (18-11) in the third game 5-1. In the fourth game it was Overall who beat Donovan 6-1, and Brown (20-6) beat Mullin 2-0 in the fifth game. The Cubs had swept the Series.

In 1908, another great year for the Cubs, they took their third straight pennant (99-55) by squeaking by the Giants. Indeed, the two teams were tied for first place at the end of the season, and this caused the first playoff game in major league history to be scheduled. The Cubs won, 4-2, and finished one game ahead.

On September 23, 1908, the Cubs had faced the Giants at the height of the pennant race. The game was tied 1-1 in the last of the ninth inning, and the Giants were starting a rally. Giants first baseman Fred Merkle was on first, with a man on third. The next batter hit a single, and the man on third came in to score. Merkle, thinking that the game was won, turned and went to the dugout without touching second base. But second baseman Johnny Evers of the Cubs called for the ball, touched second base, and the run was disallowed by the home plate umpire. Because of the crowds who were flooding the field, the game was called a tie. Forever after, baseball fanatics have remembered Merkle's boner, although many think that the ball Evers used was not the original ball that had been hit.

Just three days later, on September 26, Cub pitcher Ed Reulbach became the only pitcher in history to throw two shutouts in a double header. He beat Brooklyn 5-0 and 3-0 in the two nine-inning games.

The Cubs met the Tigers again in the World Series in 1908. Once again the Chicagoans took the Fall Classic, this time four games to one. The Cubs leaped off to a 10-6 win in the first game, with Brown (29-9) beating Ed Summers (24-12). In the second game Overall (15-11) won over Donovan (18-7) 6-1. Then Detroit came back as Mullin (17-13) won the third game over Pfiester (12-10) 8-3. Brown won the fourth game 3-0 over Summers; Overall won the fifth game 2-0 over Donovan; and the Series was over. The people of Detroit had seemed to sense the impending devastation. The last game was played in the Motor City, and only 6201 fans showed up at Bennett Field, a record low for World Series crowds.

The Cubs fell to second place (104-49) in 1909, six games behind the Pirates. But their pitching staff tied their own record (set in 1907) of 32 shutouts that season.

It was first place (104-50) again in 1910, 13 games in front of the Giants. Again the pitching was magnificent, with Brown (25-13), King Cole (20-4) and the others turning in masterly jobs. Brown performed a miracle on August 15, when he gave up 11 hits and still pitched a shutout as the Cubs beat Brooklyn 14-0.

This was the year that a piece of doggerel in a newspaper may have made future Hall of Famers out of the Cubs' double play combination – shortstop Joe Tinker to second baseman Johnny Evers to first baseman Frank Chance. Franklin Pierce Adams, a transplanted Chicagoan, was a columnist for the *New York Daily Mail*, and on a July day in 1910 he needed eight lines to fill out his column, so he wrote a poem called "Baseball's Sad Lexicon," which created a legend.

> These are the saddest of possible words
>   Tinker to Evers to Chance.
> Trio of Bear Cubs and fleeter than birds
>   Tinker to Evers to Chance.
> Thoughtlessly pricking our gonfalon
>   bubble,
> Making a Giant hit into a double,
> Words that are weighty with nothing but
>   trouble
>   Tinker to Evers to Chance.

They were not physically overwhelming (Chance weighed only 125 pounds and stood but five feet nine and, perhaps because he had been beaned so often, developed headaches and became deaf in his right ear). They were not cooperative off the field – Tinker and Evers didn't speak to each other for years. And they really weren't a fantastic double play combination. Actually, in the year of the poem, they combined for only 16 twin killings. Nevertheless, they were good enough to make the name Harry Steinfield one of the favorite trivia items for baseball fans. Steinfield, who had led the league in hits in 1906 and ended his career with a .268 batting average, was the forgotten third baseman in the Cubs' infield.

But this year the Cubs met the Philadelphia Athletics, and, with the exception of the fourth game, the World Series was a Philadelphia clinic. The Athletics won the first game 4-1, with Chief Bender (23-5) beating Overall (12-6). They took the second game, too, 9-4, Jack Coombs (31-9) beating Brown (25-13). The third game again went to the Athletics 12-5, Coombs winning over Harry McIntyre (13-9).

The fourth game finally went to the Cubs when Brown beat Bender 4-3. Philadelphia manager Connie Mack later said that he should have taken the Series in a sweep, but he let sentiment get in the way of his better judgement. With his club ahead 3-2 in the eighth inning, Mack dismissed a hunch that Topsy Hartsel should pinch hit for catcher Ira Thomas, and Thomas ruined

Above left: *Frank Chance, the Cubs' first baseman who led them to their only two World Series victories, in 1907 and 1908.*

Above: *Johnny Evers and Joe Tinker turning another of their famous double plays. They were more famous than prolific, as they turned only 16 double plays in 1910 when the famous poem was written.*

Above: *Future Hall of Fame pitcher Mordecai "Three Finger" Brown finished his career with the Cubs in 1916, the year the club moved from West Side Park to Weeghman Park. Weeghman Park was renamed Wrigley Field in the 1920s.*

Above right: *Hank O'Day was the manager of the Cubs in 1914.*

a rally by hitting into a double play with the bases loaded. The Cubs went on to score a run in the ninth and another in the tenth to win the game. Then the Athletics ended the Series in the fifth game with a 7-2 win, Coombs winning his third game to beat Brown, and the Cubs were the losers, four games to one.

The Cubs finished in second place (92-62) in 1911, seven and one-half games behind the Giants. They fell to third place (91-59) in 1912, 11½ games behind the Giants, and Chance was off to the American League to manage in New York.

In 1913 the second member of the double play combination, Johnny Evers, became the manager of the Cubs. They stayed in third place (88-65), 13½ games behind the Giants, and Evers was off to the Boston Braves as a player. The highlight of the season may have come on September 15, when pitcher Larry Cheney shut out the Giants 7-0, despite allowing 14 hits.

The new manager in 1914 was Hank O'Day, but the club slipped to fourth place (78-76) 16½ games behind the Braves. Unrealized at the time, the event that would most affect the Cubs that year was the appearance of the Federal League, a circuit that was to last only two years. Charles Weeghman, the owner of the Chicago Whales of the Federal League, opened Weeghman Park, where his team played. It

cost $250,000 and could seat 14,000. It was soon to be a part of the Cubs' tradition.

Roger Bresnahan replaced O'Day in 1915 and brought the team in in fourth place (73-80), 17½ games behind the Phillies, and he was gone. About the only highlight of the season came on June 17, when pitcher George "Zip" Zabel was called in to relieve against Brooklyn with two out in the first inning. He won 4-3 in the 19th inning in the longest relief performance in the majors.

With the collapse of the Federal League after the 1915 season, Weeghman bought the Cubs, the team moved from the old West Side Park and the final member of the double play combination of the Cubs, Joe Tinker, was brought in as manager in 1916. He could do no better than a fifth-place finish (67-86), finishing 16½ games behind Brooklyn, and was fired. But the Cubs did win their first game in Weeghman Park on April 20, beating the Reds 7-6 in 11 innings. Another first that year occurred on June 29, when the Cubs and the Reds played a complete nine-inning game and used but one baseball.

On September 14, 1916, another milestone was reached. Two of the great pitching stars of the National League — both of them future Hall of Famers — went head to head in their last appearances on a baseball field. They were Christy Mathewson and Three Finger Brown. Mathewson was then the player-manager of the Reds, and Brown had just returned to the Cubs. Meeting in Chicago, both pitchers had agreed to bow out together in the second game of a double header, and before the game each had received a bouquet of American Beauty roses. The Cubs jumped to a 2-0 lead in the bottom of the first inning, but the Reds, led at the plate by Mathewson's double and two singles, kept pecking away at Brown until they had a 10-5 lead going into the bottom of the ninth inning. At that point Matty nearly fell apart, yielding three runs, but he hung on to gain the 10-8 victory. For Mathewson it was his 373rd career win against 188 losses. For Brown the defeat was his 130th against 239 victories.

In 1917 the new manager was Fred Mitchell. He could manage only a fifth-place (74-80) finish, 24 games in back of the Giants. The highlight of this year occurred on May 2. Despite the facts that the odds against a single pitcher throwing a no-hitter are 500-1 and the chances of two pitchers doing so in the same game are 250,000-1, Fred Toney of the Reds and Jim "Hippo" Vaughn of the Cubs pitched the only double no-hitter in history, each giving up only two walks in the first nine innings. But in the top of the tenth inning

Left: *Roger Bresnahan replaced Hank O'Day as manager in 1915.*

Below: *Mordecai Brown and Christy Mathewson appeared for the last time at Weeghman Park on Labor Day 1916. Both pitchers entered the Hall of Fame soon after it was established.*

Right: *Fred Toney pitched for the Reds in the only double no-hitter in history, in 1917.* **Far right,** *his opponent in the double no-hitter was James "Hippo" Vaughn. The Cubs lost the game in the tenth inning when Vaughn gave up a hit followed by two errors.*

Opposite right: *Babe Ruth pitched for the Boston Red Sox against the Cubs in the 1918 World Series. The Cubs broke his string of 29⅔ scoreless World Series innings, a record which stood for over 40 years. Some say Ruth was a better pitcher than he ever was a hitter. But, he was quite spectacular in both departments.*

Larry Kopf of the Reds singled, went to third on a dropped fly ball and scored on an error. Toney did not give up a run in the bottom of the inning and won the game 1-0.

Mitchell brought the Cubs in in first place (84-45) in 1918, ten and one-half games in front of the Giants. The United States was at war that year, and the major leagues were ordered to suspend the season by Labor Day. Only the two championship clubs were allowed to extend their seasons in order to play the World Series. It was the Cubs against the Red Sox.

The first game of the Series was a white-knuckle affair. Manager Ed Barrow of the Sox picked Babe Ruth (13-7) to pitch, and Fred Mitchell chose Hippo Vaughn (22-10). Boston won the game 1-0 on a run in the fourth inning in this duel between left-handers. Chicago came back in the second game when Lefty Tyler (19-9) beat Joe Bush (15-15) 3-1. Tyler helped his own cause by singling in two runs in the second inning.

Vaughn was back in the third game against Carl Mays (21-13), but lost again 3-2. The fourth game, one of the more interesting in World Series history, was yet another one-run contest, as Boston came out on top 3-2. Barrow had played Ruth in

left field several times during the season, and the Babe had tied for the home run lead with 11. In this Series game Ruth started the game and went on to pitch seven and one-third scoreless innings before Chicago scored two runs in the eighth inning to tie the score. Boston countered with the go-ahead run in the eighth, Bush came in to relieve and Ruth took left field. Ruth was the winning pitcher, and reliever Phil Douglas (9-9) was the loser. Until the Cubs scored, Ruth had run up a string of 29⅔ consecutive scoreless World Series innings, a record that was not broken until 1961.

There was a sit-down strike before game five. For the first time in history the second-, third- and fourth-place teams were to receive a share in the receipts, and the Cubs and Sox players, demanding larger shares, called the strike, thus delaying the game for a time before they capitulated. The Cubs then won the game 3-0, with Vaughn beating Sad Sam Jones (16-5). The sixth game handed the championship to the Red Sox, 4-2, as Mays beat Tyler.

In 1919 it was third place (75-65) for the Cubs — 21 games behind the champion Reds. And so ended the second decade of the modern era.

3. A Dynasty Begins

For the 1920 season Weeghman Park was renamed Cubs Park, but it stayed the same as far as its dimensions were concerned – 355 feet in left field, 353 in right field and 400 feet to center field. Mitchell was able to do no better that year than fourth place (75-79), 11 games behind the first-place Giants, and he was off to become the manager of the Boston Braves. After the end of the season, when the facts of the game-fixing "Black Sox Scandal" had been made known and exposed the members of the White Sox who had sold out to the gamblers, an overwrought citizen of Joliet, Illinois, accosted second baseman Buck Herzog. He accused Herzog of being "one of those crooked Chicago players," then slashed him with a knife. Herzog was indeed a Chicago player – a Chicago Cub.

Johnny Evers was back for another go at

A band greets the arrival of the Cubs on Catalina Island where spring training took place until the 1950s, apart from the war years when they trained at French Lick, Indiana.

managing the Cubs in 1921, but he didn't last long. With a 42-56 record and the club in seventh place, he was fired two-thirds of the way through the season. The club brought in Bill Killefer to take over the reins, but he didn't do much by winning 22 and losing 33, and the Cubs ended the season in seventh place (64-89) and a horrible 30 games behind the first-place Giants.

Killefer didn't do much better in 1922, when the Cubs ended in fifth place (80-74), but this time they were only 13 games behind the first-place Giants. The high spot of the season came on August 25. In one of the wildest games ever played, the Cubs beat the Phillies 26-23. Chicago led 25-6 in the fourth inning, but they were only just able to hold on as the Phillies went down in the ninth with the bases loaded.

"Reindeer Bill" Killefer still hadn't found

place (82-72), only seven games behind the first-place Cardinals.

The Chicago fans had high hopes for their club, and in 1927 the Cubs were the first team in the National League to pass the million mark in attendance. But it was another fourth-place finish (85-68) – trailing the Pirates by eight and one-half games.

With the coming of future Hall of Fame right fielder Kiki Cuyler in 1928, the Cubs began to make their comeback. Cuyler, who had been patriotic enough to enter the United States Military Academy during World War II, hit .285 that year, and the Cubs finished third (91-63), only four games behind the Cardinals.

Left: *Joe McCarthy, one of the Cubs' great managers, led them to a pennant in 1929.*

Below: *Grover Cleveland Alexander, the Cubs' Hall of Fame pitcher, whose life was immortalized in a film in which his role was played by Cub fan and former Cub radio broadcaster, Ronald Reagan.*

the magic in 1923. The Cubs finished in fourth place (83-71), 12½ games behind the championship Giants. And in 1924 they ended with a 81-72 record, finishing in fifth place, 12 games behind the Giants. A game on June 25 seemed to symbolize their futility that year. Relief pitcher Emil Yde of the Pirates doubled in the ninth inning, tying the score, then tripled in the 14th inning to win the game.

Killefer was let go in 1925, when he had led the club to 33 wins against 42 losses, putting them in seventh place. Then Rabbit Maranville was brought in to save the club, but after a 23-30 record he had them in eighth place and was fired. The season ended with the Cubs being skippered by Moon Gibson, who went 12-14. But still the club finished in eighth place (68-86), 27½ games behind the first-place Pirates. This was the first time in the history of the Cubs that they had finished in last place.

In 1926 Cubs Park was renamed Wrigley Field in honor of Phil Wrigley, the owner of the Cubs. In addition to a new name for the stadium there was a new manager. He was Joe McCarthy, a future Hall of Fame manager. He had never played in the major leagues, but he was a perfectionist who stressed fundamentals and a stern disciplinarian. As an example, on May 22 the great Cub pitcher, Grover Cleveland Alexander, was honored on the field by the Cubs. But a month later he was off to St. Louis because of a series of run-ins with McCarthy. Alexander just didn't seem to be able to follow instructions, but, to be fair, it has been suggested that this may have been because of drinking caused by epilepsy. At any rate, McCarthy brought the club in in fourth

Right: *Future Hall of Famer Kiki Cuyler played right field for the Cubs in the late twenties and early thirties.*

Below: *Wrigley Field during the 1929 World Series played against the Philadelphia A's. Note little change has taken place, other than in the bleachers, since that time.*

Nineteen twenty-nine was a banner year for the Cubs. They finally won another pennant (98-54), their first flag since 1918. The Cubs that year featured the big bats of Cuyler (.360), Hack Wilson (.345), Rogers Hornsby (.380) and Riggs Stephenson (.362), as well as the strong arms of pitchers Charlie Root (19-6), Guy Bush (18-7) and

Pat Malone (22-10). But the World Series was to be a disappointment, for the Philadelphia Athletics had a powerhouse.

In the first game Philadelphia manager Connie Mack got off to a surprising start by using pitcher Howard Ehmke (7-2), who was not part of the regular starting pitcher rotation. Ehmke kept the Cubs off-balance with his slow stuff, struck out 13 (a Series record that stood until 1953) and won 3-1. Charlie Root (19-6) was the losing pitcher. The Athletics won the second game quite convincingly, as George Earnshaw (24-8), the winning pitcher, and Lefty Grove (20-6) combined in another 13-strikeout game and beat Pat Malone (22-10), 9-3.

The Cubs came to life in the third game, winning 3-1 behind Guy Bush (18-7), with Earnshaw the loser. The fourth game started with Root facing John Quinn (11-9). After six and a half innings Chicago seemed to have the game in its pocket, with a commanding 8-0 lead. But in the bottom of the seventh the Athletics exploded with the wildest offensive one-inning display in World Series history. Fifteen men went to the plate, and the A's scored ten runs on a total of ten hits, a walk and a hit batsman. Center fielder Mule Haas also hit an inside-the-park home run. The final score was 10-8, with the win going to reliever Ed Rommel (12-2) and the loss to Sheriff Blake (14-13), the third of five pitchers used by the Cubs in the game.

The fifth game became another horror show for the Cubs. With Chicago leading

2-0 in the bottom of the ninth inning, Malone retired pinch-hitter Walter French. Then second baseman Max Bishop singled, then scored on another Haas homer that tied the score at 2-2. Malone next retired Mickey Cochrane, the catcher. With two out, left fielder Al Simmons doubled and first baseman Jimmie Foxx was given an intentional pass. The Cubs lost another World Series when right fielder Bing Miller doubled to score Simmons for a 3-2 win. The winning pitcher was Rube Walberg (18-11) and the loser was Malone. The Athletics had won the Series, four games to one.

Nineteen thirty was a strange year. The club had slumped to third place (85-64) when owner Phil Wrigley fired McCarthy with one week to go in the season because he had not won the pennant. McCarthy was to go on to manage the Yankees for many successful years. Rogers Hornsby was brought in to finish the season, and he won four while losing none, bringing the Cubs in in second place (90-64), only two games behind the Cardinals. That year the Cubs set a new home attendance record of 1,463,264.

Hornsby was a great baseball player. As an infielder, he had won the triple crown twice, and he held the National League record for most batting titles won in a row, six. He even guarded his eyesight by not going to the movies because he thought they flickered. But he was also one of the most arrogant and tactless men in a game not noted for its refined etiquette. His record of playing for five different teams and managing five different clubs was directly attributable to the inability of any owner, manager or player to put up with his "frankness," even when he was winning.

Hard-drinking center fielder Hack Wilson had his finest year in 1930. That year Wilson came into his own with 208 hits – 35 of them doubles, six of them triples and 56 of them home runs. He scored 146 runs,

belted in 190 runs and hit for a .356 average. He also led the league in walks and strikeouts and registered 423 total bases, with an awesome .723 slugging percentage. His 56 homers are still the National League record, and his 190 RBIs are the major league record.

Hornsby was able only to finish third (84-70) in 1931, 17 games behind the league-leading Cardinals. About the only thing positive about that season was that the Cubs bought future Hall of Fame second baseman Billy Herman from Dayton of the Central League for $60,000.

In 1932, with the Cubs in second place (53-44), Hornsby was fired on August 2 after a series of vitriolic policy disputes with club president William Veeck, Sr. The next year he was managing the St. Louis Browns. It was Charlie "Jolly Cholly" Grimm who was brought in to finish the season. He recorded a 37-20 mark, enough to put the Cubs in first place (90-64). At the end of the season the Cubs' players, who really hated Hornsby, voted him no share in the World Series money.

The 1932 World Series was a Chicago disaster, even an embarrassment. It was also the year of Joe McCarthy's revenge. He had been seemingly senselessly dismissed as manager of the Cubs late in the 1930 season, and now he was the manager of the Yankees, bringing them in in first place (107-47) in the American League, 13 games ahead of the Athletics. Not only was McCarthy understandably upset with the Cubs, but the whole Yankee team was angry, too, because of the way Chicago had treated one of their old teammates, Mark Koenig. Shortstop Koenig had arrived in Chicago late in the season, playing 33

Above left: *Pictured left to right are William Wrigley Jr., Cub owner, Joe McCarthy, manager, and Bill Veeck Sr., general manager of the team in 1929. A few years later Bill Veeck's son helped plant the vines which adorn the outfield walls at Wrigley Field.*

Below: *Hack Wilson at bat at Wrigley Field in 1930, the year in which he drove in 190 runs, a record which may never be broken.*

games and batting .353, with a slugging average of .510. Actually, he had been one of the prime reasons that the Cubs had won the pennant. But he was voted only a quarter of a share of the World Series money.

The first two games were played at Yankee Stadium. In the first game Guy Bush of the Cubs (19-11) faced Red Ruffing (18-7), and for three innings it looked good for Chicago, since they had scored two runs in the top of the first. Then the Yankees scored three runs in the fourth, five runs in the sixth, three runs in the seventh and one run in the eighth, to win 12-6 – all this on a mere ten hits. The second game was a little closer, with the Yankees winning only 5-2, with Lefty Gomez (24-7) beating Lon Warneke (22-6) but giving up ten hits to nine.

The Cubs looked a little better in the

Above right: *Charlie Grimm, manager of the Cubs, shakes hands with Joe McCarthy, ex-Cub manager and now New York Yankee manager, before the opening game of the 1932 World Series at Yankee Stadium. McCarthy got his revenge by beating the Cubs four straight.*

Right: *Program from the 1932 World Series.*

YANKEES vs CUBS

WORLD'S SERIES OFFICIAL PROGRAM 25¢

YANKEE STADIUM·1932

HARRY M. STEVENS, INC., Publisher

Above: *The first game of the 1932 World Series at Yankee Stadium. Note that the Yankees' number four, Lou Gehrig, has just gotten a base hit in the first of four Cubs losses.*

third game in Chicago, even being able to tie it up 4-4 in the fourth inning. But the Yankees went on to win it 7-5, with George Pipgras (16-9) beating Charlie Root (15-10). It was in this game that an historic event took place. In the top half of the fifth inning, with the score tied 4-4, right fielder Babe Ruth came to the plate. At that point a fan threw a lemon at him. It missed, but the crowd laughed. Ruth stepped back into the box to face Root. The first pitch was a strike, and as the fans cheered, Ruth stepped back and pointed toward center field. The next pitch was a strike, and the Babe repeated his gesture. Then came two balls. Finally, the Bambino hit the next pitch into the stands at a point exactly where he had pointed. First baseman Lou Gehrig followed with another homer, and the Yanks went on to win the game.

Did he mean to indicate that he was going to hit a roundtripper? No one will ever know. He did hold up one finger after the first strike and two fingers after the second strike. But after those gestures did he also point to center field? Cub catcher Gabby Hartnett claimed that he didn't. Yankee manager Joe McCarthy didn't see it, nor did pitcher Root. It was not mentioned in the newspapers the next day. The idea didn't surface in the press until three days after the game. Years later a home

movie was examined that seemed to indicate that Ruth was pointing at something, but the trajectory seemed to say that it was at Root or the Cubs' dugout, not the center-field fence. Good legends die hard, however, especially since this was to be the Bambino's last World Series homer.

Chicago fans were cheered for a time in the fourth game when the Cubs scored four runs in the first inning and went ahead by a score of 4-1. Then the Yankees began to apply their version of the Chinese water torture by scoring two runs in the third, two in the sixth, four in the seventh and four in the ninth. The final score was 13-6. The winner was Wilcy Moore (10-2), and the loser was Jakie May (2-2), both in relief. The ignominious four-game sweep was over.

The Cubs slipped to third (86-68) in 1933, six games behind the first-place Giants. And it was third again (86-65) in 1934, trailing the pennant-winning Cardinals by eight games.

But the Cubs had the power again in 1935, with pitchers Lon Warneke and Bill Lee winning 20 games, and second baseman Billy Herman, third baseman Stan Hack, center fielder Frank Demaree, left fielder Augie Galan and catcher Gabby Hartnett all hitting over .300. Hartnett also won the National League's Most

Above: *A painting showing Babe Ruth calling his shot in the third game of the 1932 World Series at Wrigley Field. The event may not have happened exactly this way, but the pitcher who delivered the go-fer ball, Charlie Root, never recovered from the shock of it all.*

Above right: *Charlie Root was a fine right-hander for the Cubs, but neither he nor the Cubs were a match for the great 1932 Yankee team.*

Valuable Player Award. Manager Grimm brought the team in in first place (100-54), four games ahead of the Cardinals. Along the way, Galan set a major league record on September 29 by playing in his 154th game without hitting into a double play.

The Cubs met the Tigers in the World Series. Chicago had lost its previous four Series and Detroit had done the same. The question was, who would break the jinx? The Cubs had won the pennant with an amazing 21-game winning streak in September, and, buoyed by their momentum, they took the first game of the Series 3-0 as Warneke (20-13) pitched a four-hitter to defeat Schoolboy Rowe (19-13). But the Bengals had no trouble with the Cubs in the second game, beating them 8-3, after handing winner Tommy Bridges (21-10) a four-run lead in the first inning. Charlie Root (15-8) was the loser. In the third game of the Series Detroit scored the winning run in the ninth inning. Rowe won this one 6-5, beating Larry French (17-10). But Detroit suffered a potentially fatal loss in the game when first baseman Hank Greenberg, the Most Valuable Player in the American League that year, broke his wrist.

Still, Detroit increased its lead, three games to one, in the fourth game by winning 2-1 behind General Crowder (16-10), who threw a five-hitter to beat Charlie Root. Chicago came back in the fifth game with a 3-1 victory when Warneke beat Rowe once again. In this game the Cubs' "Arkansas Hummingbird" suffered a muscle injury, but Bill Lee (20-6) came it to relieve, holding the Tigers to four hits in the final three innings.

Bridges faced French in the sixth game, and it was a close contest. Detroit scored in the first inning, and Chicago tied it at 1-1 in the third. In the fourth the Tigers scored another run, Chicago countered with two in the fifth and the Bengals tied it again with one in the sixth. Going into the ninth, it was still deadlocked at 3-3. The Cubs' third baseman, Stan Hack, led off the inning with a triple. But Bridges took charge, striking out shortstop Billy Jurges, tossing French out at first base and retiring left fielder Augie Galan on an outfield fly. When the Tigers scored a run in the bottom

of the ninth they had won the game 4-3, and the Series four games to two.

The Cubs slipped a bit in 1936, finishing second (87-67), five games behind the Giants. And it was second (93-61) again in 1937, but this time trailing the Giants by only three games. One of the wonderful nostalgic bits was added to Wrigley Field in 1937 with the opening of the new scoreboard. It was hand-operated, and the three men who changed the scores for every major league baseball game in progress worked in the un-airconditioned sweatbox. Today it remains virtually the same, except for some modern touches such as an electronic message board. As far as trivia events in 1937 are concerned, Cubs first baseman Rip Collins played a whole game on June 29 without a single putout or assist – an almost impossible feat for a first baseman.

After 81 games into the 1938 season, and with the club at 45-36, "Jolly Cholly" Grimm, who had been called "The best banjo player in the National League," was

Below: *The 1938 National League Championship Chicago Cubs. First baseman Phil Cavarretta stands in the top row, second from the left. Shortstop Bill Jurges is fourth from the left in the second row. Second baseman Billie Herman is second from the left seated. Charlie Grimm, the manager, is seated at the center, and on his right is Gabby Hartnett, whose homer won the pennant for the Cubs. Woody English and Stan Hack sit to Charlie Grimm's left next to Lon Warneke, the Cubs' great pitcher.*

Dizzy Dean was traded to the Cubs by the Cardinals in the middle of the 1938 season, and helped the Cubs win the pennant.

Cubs, came to Chicago for a three-game series. The Pirates were so confident of winning the pennant that they had built a new press box at Forbes Field. In April the Cubs had bought the future Hall of Fame pitcher Dizzy Dean from the Cardinals for three players and $185,000. Dean, then a sore-armed shell of his former self, had been the last National League pitcher to win 30 games in one season. But he was still all heart. In the first game of the series with the Pirates, Dizzy beat Pittsburgh 2-1. As he himself said, "It's only bragging when you say you're going to do something and then can't do it."

The next day was the one in which the future Hall of Famer Harnett got the hit that made him an immortal. It was a dark afternoon on September 28 when Clay Bryant, the 19-game winner, started for Chicago and Bob Klinger (12-5) started for Pittsburgh. As the lead seesawed back and forth, a total of nine pitchers trudged to the mound. In the top of the eighth inning the Pirates finally took the lead, 5-3, but the Cubs came back in the bottom of the eighth, adding two more runs before they were stopped by fireman Mace Brown and a brilliant defensive play by right fielder Paul Waner, whose masterly throw cut down the tie-breaking run at the plate.

Darkness was descending, and it was getting hard to see, but the umpires decided to let the teams play one more inning. If the score remained tied, a replay would be scheduled for the next day, an eventuality that would have been a distinct disadvantage to the Cubs. They would have had to play a double header, and their pitching staff was worn out. In any event, Cubs pitcher Charlie Root retired the Pirates with no trouble in the top of the ninth. Then Mace Brown put out the first two Cubs he faced.

The next man up was Hartnett, who swung at Brown's first pitch and missed. The next pitch was a curve ball, and Gabby fouled it off. The count was 0-2, and the third pitch came in. Harnett, barely able to see in the bad light, connected for a booming home run, a roundtripper that would be immortalized as the "Homer in the Gloamin'." He later said, "I don't think I walked a step to the plate. I was carried in."

Now a game up, the Cubs trounced the dispirited Pirates 10-1 the next day to win the pennant again in their weird three-year pennant schedule.

The Cubs had to face the Yankees again in the World Series, and later manager Joe McCarthy was to call the 1938 Yanks the greatest team he ever fielded. In the first game Cub ace pitcher Bill Lee (22-9) faced Red Ruffing (21-7). The Yankees scored two

let go. His replacement was catcher Gabby Hartnett, who became player-manager. Oddly enough, he was never called "Gabby" by his teammates, who referred to him as "Leo," his real middle name.

Less flatteringly, he was also called "Old Tomato Face." Hartnett finished the season with a 44-27 mark, and the Cubs won the pennant (89-63), nosing out the Pirates. And it was Hartnett himself who won the flag.

Late in the season Pittsburgh, leading the league with a one game bulge over the runs in the second inning and played a fine defensive game to beat Chicago 3-1. Dean (7-1) frightened New York and Lefty Gomez (18-12) for a time in the second game, as he held the Yanks to two runs on his nothing ball for seven innings, with the Cubs ahead 3-2. Then things fell apart. In the eighth inning, Yankee left fielder George Selkirk singled. After Myril Hoag batted for Gomez and forced Selkirk, shortstop Frankie Crosetti hit a home run. In the ninth, it was center fielder Joe DiMaggio who contributed a two-run homer, and Gomez had won his sixth World Series game 6-3, tying him with Hall of Fame pitchers Chief Bender and Waite Hoyt.

It was all downhill for the Cubs after that. They lost 5-2 in the third game, in which Clay Bryant (19-11) lost to Monte Pearson (16-7). The fourth game was worse.

Chicago lost 8-3, with Ruffing once again beating Lee. It was another four-game sweep of the Cubs by the Yankees.

It was about this time that a couple of Cubs made statements that few knew were harbingers of a revolution that was to occur in just nine years when Jackie Robinson broke the color barrier in the major leagues. Gabby Harnett pointed out that "If managers were given permission, there'd be a mad rush to sign up Negroes." And pitcher Dizzy Dean commented, "I have played against a Negro All-Star team that was so good we didn't think we had an even chance against them."

Nineteen thirty-nine was a downer, with the Cubs finishing in fourth place (84-70), 13 games behind the pennant-winning Reds. Then began a period that was more famine than feast.

Hartnett's Homer With 2 Out in 9th Beats Pirates

CUBS HALT PIRATES FOR 9TH IN ROW, 6-5

34,465 See Chicago Supplant Losers in League Lead With a Half-Game Advantage

ROOT WINS IN RELIEF ROLE

Lazzeri's Pinch Double Helps Tie Score in Eighth—Rizzo Connects for Corsairs

By The Associated Press.
CHICAGO, Sept. 28.—In the thickening gloom, with the score tied and two out in the ninth inning today, red-faced Gabby Hartnett blasted a home run before 34,465 cheering fans to give his Cubs a dramatic 6-to-5 victory over the Pirates and a half-game lead in

and no balls, probably saved the Cub pennant chances. Had he failed, the game would have been called because of darkness, necessitating a double bill tomorrow which would have almost insurmountably handicapped the overtaxed Cub pitching staff.

The Chicago manager, whose team was nine games out of first place a little more than a month ago, had to fight his way through a swirling, hysterical mob to touch all the bases and had trouble reaching the dugout. He called the victory and his homer "the two greatest things that ever happened to me."

Bryant Driven to Cover

A hit and two errors helped the Cubs to a run in the second and, with Clay Bryant pitching masterfully, they stayed in front until the sixth. Then the Pirates, combining Johnny Rizzo's twenty-first homer of the season with two other hits and a pair of walks, chased Bryant with a three-run blast. Jack Russell replaced him.

The Bruins came roaring right back to tie the score in their half of the inning on doubles by Hartnett and Rip Collins and a bunt which Billy Jurges beat out.

In the seventh a furiously disputed double play pulled the Cubs

Times Wide World
Gabby Hartnett

yesterday's game, went in for French and was greeted by Lee Handley's single which scored Suhr. Manush was nailed at the plate

the play Joe Marty, running for Lazzeri, was out at the plate. Paul Waner to Todd. Mace Brown replaced Swift and forced Frank Demaree to hit into a double play.

Charlie Root pitched for the Cubs in the ninth and held the Pirates to a single by Paul Waner. Phil Cavarretta and Carl Reynolds were easy outs before Hartnett won the battle and put his team on top for the first time since June 8. It was the Cubs' ninth straight victory and their nineteenth in their last twenty-two games.

Tomorrow, in the concluding game of a thrill-packed series, Lee will be Hartnett's pitching hope, with the jittery Pirates banking on Russ Bauers.

The box score:

PITTSBURGH (N.)	ab. r. h. po. a. e.		CHICAGO (N.)	ab. r. h. po. a. e.
L. Waner, cf	5 0 2 1 0 0		Hack, 3b	3 0 0 3 1 0
P. Waner, rf	5 0 2 3 1 1		Herman, 2b	5 0 3 2 2 0
Rizzo, lf	4 1 1 1 0 0		Demaree, rf	4 0 0 3 0 0
Vaughan, ss	5 2 2 1 3 5		Cavarretta, lf	5 0 0 2 0 0
Suhr, 1b	3 2 1 5 0 0		Reynolds, cf	5 0 1 5 0 0
Young, 2b	2 0 0 1 1 0		Hartnett, c	4 2 2 4 1 0
aManush	1 0 1 0 0 0		Collins, 1b	4 1 2 8 5 0 0
Thevenow, 2b	0 0 0 1 3 0		Jurges, ss	3 1 1 4 1 0
Handley, 3b	3 0 2 2 1 1		Bryant, p	2 0 1 0 0 0
Todd, c	4 0 0 2 1 1		Russell, p	0 0 0 0 0 0
Klinger, p	4 0 0 0 3 0		bO'Dea	1 0 0 0 0 0
Swift, p	0 0 0 0 0 0		Page, p	0 0 0 0 0 0
Brown, p	0 0 0 0 0 0		French, p	0 0 0 0 0 0
			Lee, p	0 0 0 0 1 0
Total	35 5 10 26 18 6		cLazzeri	1 0 1 0 0 0
			dMarty	0 0 0 0 0 0
			Root, p	0 0 0 0 0 0 0
			Total	38 6 12 27 9 0

*Two out when winning run scored.
aBatted for Young in sixth.
bBatted for Russell in sixth.
cBatted for Lee in eighth.
dRan for Lazzeri in eighth.

Pittsburgh .... 0 0 0 0 0 3 0 2 0—5
Chicago .... 0 1 0 0 0 2 0 2 1—6

Runs batted in—Manush, Rizzo, Handley 2,

Above left: *Gabby Hartnett's "homer in the Gloamin'" helped win the pennant for the Cubs in 1938. Although 34,000 saw the game, hundreds of thousands claimed they saw this home run. In fact, almost no one saw it as it disappeared into the darkness.*

Below left: *Gabby Hartnett being mobbed by Cubs fans despite his usher escort after he hit his ninth-inning home run.*

4. The Dynasty Ends

Nineteen forty was another downer, even worse than the year before. Hartnett's Cubs slipped only one spot, to fifth place, but they played below .500 ball (75-79) and finished a dreadful 25½ games behind the pennant-winning Reds. Hartnett virtually benched himself, catching in only 37 games. The team had only two winning pitchers – Claude Passeau (20-13) and Vern Olsen (13-9). True, right fielder Bill "Swish" Nicholson did hit 25 home runs, and third baseman Stan Hack hit .317, but it was still a miserable season. Hartnett was fired and left to play for the Giants.

Things got worse in 1941 when Jimmie Wilson came to manage the club. He had been the skipper of the Phillies from 1934 to 1938, and he brought the Cubs in in sixth place (70-84), this time 30 games behind the Dodgers, who won the pennant. This year only Olsen had a winning record, a pathetic 10-8, and Hack, once again hitting .317, was the only man to hit over .300. Perhaps one of the reasons for the collapse was the departure of the great second baseman, Billy Herman, who, after a mere 11 games, was sold to the Dodgers.

Nineteen forty-two found the country at

Bill "Swish" Nicholson was one of the Cubs' biggest hitters in the 1940s, and was as famous for his strikeouts as he was for his home runs. In 1943 and 1944, Swish led the league in round-trippers and runs batted in.

war. Baseball, as in World War I, was classified as a non-essential industry. In sharp contrast to the "work or fight" orders of the First World War, however, the official government policy was to encourage the game. Early in 1942, in response to a query from Baseball Commissioner Kenesaw Mountain Landis, President Franklin D. Roosevelt wrote his famous "Green Light" letter praising baseball for its contribution to national morale. "I honestly feel that it would be best for the country to keep baseball going . . . Carry on to the fullest extent consistent with the primary purpose of winning the war."

Cynics wondered if the Cubs were raising morale on 1942, since they stayed in sixth place (68-86), finishing 38 games behind the first-place Cardinals. Only pitcher Claude Passeau (19-14) had a winning record, and only the reliable Hack and left fielder Lou "The Mad Russian" Novikoff shone at the plate – each hitting an even .300. Lowlights of the 1942 season included

the time when a pitcher – Jim Tobin of the Boston Braves – hit three consecutive home runs off Cubs pitchers, Boston winning 6-5. And then there was the day when Cubs shortstop Lennie Merullo committed four errors – in a single inning.

But apparently baseball did help the national morale, because before the 1943 season ballplayers were even permitted to leave essential winter factory jobs to report for spring training. Wilson was, however, able to come up with only a token improvement in the club. He brought them in in fifth (74-79), 29½ games out of first place. But at least Passeau (15-12) had company in the winning column when Hi Bithorn won 18 while losing 12. The batting improved a bit, too, as left fielder Ival Goodman hit .320, Nicholson hit .309 and two players, first baseman Phil Cavarretta and center fielder Peanuts Lowrey, were in the .290s.

Phil Wrigley was disgusted with Wilson's performance as manager, and in 1944, after ten games and the team at 1-9, he fired

A sight many Cub fans believed they'd never see again: the Wrigley Field sign at the corner of Clark and Addison showing the Cubs as National League champions during the opening of the 1945 World Series. Note the Clark Street car in the background.

Above: *In 1945 Phil Cavarretta led the Cubs and the league in batting, with .355, and won the Most Valuable Player Award.*

Right: *Paul Derringer was one of the leaders of the Cubs' winning pitching staff in their last winning season in 1945.*

the skipper. Roy Johnson, a former outfielder, was brought in as interim manager for one game, which he lost. Wrigley then brought in his former manager, Charlie Grimm, to finish the season. Grimm was able to turn the team around a bit, winning 74 and losing 69, and was to return the next year in triumph. The Cubs finally finished in fourth place (75-79) in 1944, 30 games behind the first-place Cardinals, and Passeau (15-9) had another pitcher to join him in the winners' circle, Hank Wyse (16-15). Cavarretta led the team, with a .321 average, and left fielder Dom Dallessandro hit .304.

The Cubs got a lucky break when right-fielding superstar Stan Musial of the Cardinals entered the Navy after the 1944 season. St. Louis had won the pennant for three straight years, and Musial was their mainstay, hitting .315, .357 and .347 and fielding brilliantly. Nineteen forty-five was the last of the war years, and most clubs were still fielding teams of young boys, older men, 4-Fs and married men with several children.

At that point the Cubs were the cream of the crop in the National League, spearheaded by Cavarretta and pitcher Hank Borowy. Cavarretta led the league in hitting, with a .355 average, and he batted in 97 runs on his way to becoming the choice for Most Valuable Player in the National League. Borowy had come to the Cubs in July and had promptly gone 11-2, with one save. Third baseman Stan Hack hit .323, and second baseman Don Johnson hit an uncharacteristic .302 (his career batting average was .273).

The pitching was magnificent. In addition to Borowy, whose earned run average of 2.13 led the league, six Cub pitchers had winning records – Hank Wyse (22-11), Claude Passeau (17-9, with one save), Paul Derringer (16-11, with four saves), Ray Prim (13-8, with two saves), Paul Erickson (7-4, with three saves) and Hy Vandenburg (6-3, with two saves).

The Cubs edged out the Cardinals on the next to the last day of the season, ending at 98-56, three games ahead. It was to be their last championship of any kind for 39 years. In the American League it was the Detroit Tigers, who also had a battle, winning the flag over the Washington Senators on the last day of the season. Because of the wartime lineups, sportswriter Warren Brown of *The Chicago Tribune* wrote: "I don't think either team can win." But it turned out to be one of the most exciting World Series ever.

In the first game Borowy posted a shutout over Tigers pitcher Hal Newhouser (25-9), who was relieved in the third inning by the first of three other pitchers. The Cubs, after scoring four runs in the top of the first inning, went on to win 9-0, with Borowy scattering six hits. In the second game Virgil Trucks (0-0), out of the Navy for less than a week, beat Wyse 4-1 on a three-run home

Left: *The 1945 National League champion Chicago Cubs. Bottom left is Andy Pafko, Charlie Grimm is third from left in the second row, and Clyde McCullough is next to him. Sixth from the right in the back row is Peanuts Lowery.*

Below: *Happy Cub fans in the bleachers join Detroit fans in Briggs Stadium for the third game of the 1945 World Series.*

Andy Pafko was out at second, but Hank Greenberg could not catch Skeeter Webb's wild throw to first base for the double play in the second game of the 1945 World Series. The batter, Mickey Livingston, was nabbed at second when he tried to take two. The umpire at first is Jacques O'Conlin.

run in the fifth inning by outfielder Hank Greenberg, also just out of the service.

Passeau of the Cubs pitched a masterpiece in the third game. It was a one-hitter, the only blow being a single by first baseman Rudy York in the second inning. Passeau walked only one man, and since both Tigers runners were erased in double plays, he faced only the minimum 27 men in what was the greatest World Series pitching feat up to that time. The Cubs won 3-0, the loser being Stubby Overmire (9-9). Then, in the fourth game, it was Detroit's turn again. Dizzy Trout threw a five-hitter at the Cubs, beating Prim 4-1. In the fifth game Newhouser struck out nine Cubs, and Greenberg laced three doubles for an 8-4 victory over Borowy. Chicago came back to tie the Series in the sixth game. This one was a box score nightmare. Nineteen players were used by each team. After five innings the Cubs were ahead by a comfortable 4-1 score, but in the sixth inning Detroit third baseman Jimmy Outlaw hit a hard smash to the mound that ripped the nail off the middle finger of the right hand of the pitcher – Passeau – who had to leave the game in the seventh. Detroit scored four runs in the eighth, tying the game 7-7. The Cubs finally scored in the twelfth inning to win 8-7, with Borowy, in relief, the winner.

The final game was a disaster for the Cubs, beginning when the Bengals scored five runs in the top of the first. Borowy, who had appeared in the previous two games, was simply too tired. He failed to retire a single batter, giving up a quick run on successive singles by shortstop Skeeter Webb, second baseman Eddie Mayo and center

fielder Roger Kramer. The horrible inning continued with Derringer in relief. Greenberg sacrificed, and right fielder Roy Cullenbine was intentionally walked. Outlaw was unintentionally walked, which forced in a run. Then catcher Paul Richards cleaned the bases with a double, and the Tigers kept their lead until the end. Newhouser won the game 9-3, and the Tigers took the Series four games to three.

Perhaps because they were demoralized the Cubs fell to third place (82-71) in 1946, 14½ games behind the first-place Cardinals. Only first baseman Eddie Waitkus (.304) was over .300, and, although five pitchers had winning records – Wyse (14-12), Borowy (12-10), Erickson (9-7), Passeau (9-8) and Emil Kush (9-2) – they were not sensational records. Perhaps the highlight of that futile season occurred on September 15 in Brooklyn's Ebbetts Field. The Dodgers beat the Cubs 2-0 in a game that was called after five innings because of gnats.

The Cubs deepened their tailspin in 1947, falling to sixth (69-85), 25 games out of first. True, Cavaretta, playing left field, did hit .314, and center fielder Andy Pafko hit .302, but the best pitching record on the club was Kush's 8-3, with Doyle Lade's 11-10 being the next best. Star pitcher Johnny Schmitz led the league in losses, with 18.

The bottom-of-the-barrel year was 1948. The Cubs finished last (64-90), 27½ games behind the Boston Braves. Schmitz had a barely acceptable year at 18-13, and pitcher Jess Dobernick went 7-2, but they were the only winning pitchers. Pafko (.312) and catcher Bob Scheffing (.300) led the team in hitting, but still it was eighth place – only the second time in their 72-year history in the National League that the Cubs had finished last. Owner Wrigley was appalled and took out full-page ads in the Chicago newspapers apologizing to the Cub fans and vowing this would never happen again. But of course it did.

Indeed, it happened the very next year, 1949. With the Cubs in last place (19-30), Grimm was let go. (He was to resurface as the manager of the Boston Braves.) Frankie Frisch was brought in to lead the club, but he could do no better than 42-62, and the team ended in eighth place again (61-93), 36 games behind the Brooklyn Dodgers. Perhaps their only moment in the sun came on October 2, when the Cardinals had to use nine pitchers against them in a nine-inning game, a major league record.

In a small way 1950 was an improvement: at least Frisch brought the Cubs in in seventh place (64-89). But they were 16½ half games behind the first-place Phillies, who were called "The Whiz Kids," since their average age was only 26. The Cubs' hitting was weak, with only old reliable Andy Pafko (.304) and outfielder Hank

Edwards (.364) batting over .300. The problem was illustrated by the fact that, of the rest of the starting lineup, Hank Sauer, at .274, had the best batting average. And the pitching was atrocious. Only Frank Hiller (12-5) and Dutch Leonard (5-1) had winning records. Bob Rush, the star of the pitching staff, went 13-20 and led the league in losses. From there down it was Johnny Schmitz (10-16), Paul Minner (8-13), Monk Dubiel (6-10), Doyle Lade (5-6) and Johnny Klippstein (2-9). It was a wonder that the club didn't finish last again.

But last they were in 1951. After 80 games, with the Bruins at 35-45, Frisch was fired. The man who inherited his job was the idol of Chicago, the Most Valuable Player in the glory year of 1945, Phil Cavarretta. The fans cheered, since Cavarretta was a native son, but he couldn't do much, leading the team to a 27-47 record and bringing them in in eighth place (62-92 overall), 34½ games behind the first-place Giants. This, it could be argued, was the worst team in Cubs history. True, good old Dutch Leonard was their best pitcher, with a 10-6 record. Equally true, rookie pitcher Bob Kelly went 7-4. But the rest of the pitchers were terrible. Consider: Bob Rush

Below left: *Charlie Grimm managed the Cubs 14 years and won the pennant with them in 1932, 1935, 1938 and 1945.*

Below: *Andy Pafko, the kid from Boyceville, Wisconsin, led the Cubs in the 1945 World Series. When Pafko was traded to the Brooklyn Dodgers in 1951, Cubs fans' hearts were broken.*

Above: *New Cubs manager Frankie Frisch talks with his first baseman Phil Cavarretta in the dugout in June of 1949. Frankie Frisch took over the job from Charlie Grimm, but the Cubs still kept losing.*

Right: *One of the greatest trades in Cubs history was the acquisition of Hank Saver in 1949, who came from the Cincinnati Reds with Frankie Baumholtz for Harry "The Hat" Walker and Peanuts Lowrey. Saver won the Most Valuable Player Award in 1952.*

(11-12), Paul Minner (6-17 and leading the league in losses), Cal McLish (4-10), Frank Hiller (6-12), Turk Lown (4-9) and Johnny Klippstein (6-6). Then there were the hitters, and some might say, "What hitters?" Only first baseman-manager Cavarretta himself was of any help. He hit .311, way above his career average of .283. But following him, 30 points back, was the teams' second best hitter, outfielder Gene Hermanski. First baseman Chuck Connors, who was later to turn actor and star in the TV series "The Rifleman" and as one of the villains in the miniseries "Roots," hit .239. And he was one of the better men at the plate. Second baseman Wayne Terwilliger hit .214, and shortstop Jack Cusick batted .177.

The Cubs were able to climb up to fifth place (77-77), 19½ games behind Brooklyn, in 1952, and at least they broke even. They even had three pitchers with winning records – Rush (17-13), Warren Hacker (15-9) and Minner (14-9). Of course, right fielder Frankie Baumholtz (.325) and first baseman Dee Fondy (.300) broke the .300 barrier, and that helped. The team also had a little bit of luck. For example, on June 14 the great Boston Braves pitcher Warren Spahn struck out 18 Cubs in a 15-inning game but still lost the game 3-1. One unusual thing about the season was that Hank Sauer, the teams' left fielder, won the

Most Valuable Player Award in the National League. Sauer had batted only .270, but he had led the league with 37 home runs and 121 runs batted in. Nevertheless, this caused a controversy. Never before had a team so low in the standings supplied the league with a Most Valuable Player. But Sauer had commited only six errors in the course of making 327 putouts, and he had a .983 fielding average.

In 1953 the Cubs tried to improve themselves by getting future Hall of Famer Ralph Kiner from the Pirates 41 games into the season. Kiner, the left fielder who once said, "Home run hitters drive Cadillacs, singles hitters drive Fords," did hit 28 roundtrippers in 117 games. But of course that wasn't enough, and the Cubs finished seventh (65-89), trailing the Dodgers by a horrible 40 games. Only pitcher Turk Lown (8-7) won more games than he lost. The rest of the pitching squad looked like this: Hacker (12-19, and leading the league in losses), Minner (12-15), Klippstein (10-11), Rush (9-14), Howie Pollet (5-6), Bubba Church (4-5) and Dutch Leonard (2-3). The batting wasn't all that bad, with first baseman Dee Fondy hitting .309 and Frankie Baumholtz coming in at .306. But the fielding was miserable. The Cubs' regulars

Cub outfielder Ralph Kiner hits his second home run in one game against the New York Giants at the Polo Grounds in June 1953. Kiner and Saver made a hard-hitting combination in the outfield – that was the good news. The bad news was that neither one could field any hit more than three feet away from them.

made 119 errors that year, and second baseman Eddie Miksis, with his 23 errors, helped some wag to come up with a variation of the famous "Tinker to Evers to Chance" poem. Fondy, of course, was on first, and Roy Smalley was at shortstop, and the poem was titled "Miksis to Smalley to Grandstand." Manager Phil Cavarretta was fired, and he left to finish his career playing for the White Sox. After all, he was a home-town boy, and still a favorite in Chicago. It turned out that he had some life left, for he hit .316 for the Sox in 1954.

Former Cub legend Stan Hack took over the reins as manager in 1954. But the club stayed right where it had been the year before – in seventh place (64-90), this time 33 games behind the Giants. The team had only one winning pitcher again, Jim Davis (11-7). The rest of the pitching roster had a bad year – Bob Rush (13-15), Paul Minner (11-11), Warren Hacker (6-13), Johnny Klippstein (4-11), Howie Pollet (8-10), Hal Jeffcoat (5-6) and Dave Cole (3-8). Only catcher Walker Cooper (.310) was able to break the .300 batting average barrier, but he had come from the Pirates late in the season and played only 57 games for Chicago. Right fielder Hank Sauer batted .288. Tied for third place in the hitting column were left fielder Ralph Kiner and first baseman Dee Fondy, both with .285. The only good thing on the horizon for the

Cubs, although they didn't know it at the time, was that they had more than one future Hall of Famer on the team. It seemed logical that Kiner would one day make the Hall, but few suspected that the young shortstop, Ernie Banks, would become a superstar. He had come up the year before but had played only ten games. In 1954 he hit .275 and had 19 home runs, just three fewer than slugger Kiner. Other than that, the team was a disaster, except that the Cubs did have the wittiest catcher in the majors playing for them – a fellow named Joe Garagiola.

Hack was able to bring the team in in sixth place (72-81) in 1955, trailing the Dodgers by 26 games. It was a slight improvement, and at least they had three pitchers who were over .500 – Bob Rush (13-11), Hal Jeffcoat (8-6) and Howie Pollet (4-3). Minner was 9-9, and the others all had negative statistics – Sam "Toothpick" Jones (14-20), Warren Hacker (11-15) and Jim Davis (7-11). Perhaps the biggest pitching disappointment was Jones. He had looked good early in the season and had even pitched one of the toughest no-hit, no-run games in history on May 12. On that day he faced the Pirates in Wrigley Field, and in the ninth inning he walked the bases full. Then he took a deep breath and struck out the next three batters to win 4-0. But Jones then went on to lead the league in losses. Besides the pitching mediocrity, not a single Cub hit in the .300s, as Banks led the regulars on the team with a .295.

It was last place (60-94) in 1956, 33 games behind first-place Brooklyn. About the only interesting thing that happened that year occurred on May 2, when the Cubs and Giants combined to set a record for the most pinch hitters used by both teams in a single game: each club sent seven pinch hitters to the plate in this 17-inning game. Strange as it may seem, there were three pitchers who won more games than they lost, Rush (13-10), Lown (9-8) and Vito Valentinetti (6-4). But Jones (9-14), Hacker (3-13), Don Kaiser (4-9), Davis (5-7) and Jim Brosnan (5-9) all were losers. And the batting didn't improve. Once again, no one hit .300 or more.

Banks led the club, with .297, and right fielder Walt Moryn hit .285, but the rest of the lineup consisted of weak hitters. After the season Hack was fired. He would go on to manage the Cardinals in 1958.

The Cubs called on their old catcher, Bob Scheffing, to take over the club in 1957. He was able to bring the team up to seventh place (62-92), but 33 games behind the first-place Milwaukee Braves. Of the pitchers, only rookie Dick Drott, at 15-11, had a winning record, while Brosnan went 5-5. Then it was downhill, with second-year-man Moe Drabowsky (13-15), Rush (6-16), Don Elston (6-7), Dave Hillman (6-11) and Lown (5-7). There was finally a .300 hitter, as first baseman Dale Long hit .305, and the overall batting improved somewhat, with three

In 1954 the hard-hitting Cubs were joined by rookie shortstop and future Hall of Famer Ernie Banks, who hit 19 home runs that year. Banks poses with manager Stan Hack after hitting his fortieth home run in 1955, breaking the major-league record for homers by a shortstop.

men in the .280s – right fielder Walt Moryn (.289), center fielder Chuck Tanner and shortstop Ernie Banks (.285).

Nineteen fifty-eight represented quite an improvement. The Cubs came in in fifth place (72-82) and were only 20 games behind the first-place Braves. Three pitchers had winning records – second-year man Glen Hobbie (10-6), Elston (9-8) and Bill Henry (5-4). In addition, Johnny Briggs registered a 5-5 record. Otherwise, it was Taylor Phillips (7-10), Drott (7-11), Hillman (4-8) and Drabowsky (9-11). Two men hit over .300, shortstop Banks (.313) and right fielder Lee Walls (.304). Other respectable hitters were third baseman Alvin Dark (.295), center fielder Bobby Thomson (.283) and first baseman Dale Long (.271). The best thing to happen that year was the naming of Ernie Banks as the Most Valuable Player in the National League, despite the fact that he played for a fifth-place team. In addition to hitting .313, he led the league in times at bat (617), home runs (47) and runs batted in (129).

It was another fifth-place finish (74-80) in 1959, but this time they were only 13 games behind first-place Los Angeles. Three pitchers had winning records this year – Hobbie (16-13), Henry (9-8) and Elston (10-8). Art Ceccarelli broke even at 5-5, and the rest of the roster went like this: Bob Anderson (12-13), Hillman (8-11), Drabowsky (5-10), Jim Buzhardt (4-5). Utility outfielder Irv Noren led the team in batting, with a .321 mark, and Banks hit .304. For the first time in National League history a player won the Most Valuable Player Award two years in a row when Ernie Banks was honored again. Not only did he hit .304, he led the league in runs batted in (143), assists (519) and fielding average (.985).

But skipper Bob Scheffing was dropped at the end of the season. He was to resurface as Tigers manager in 1961.

Opposite: *Ernie Banks hits another home run. He won the Most Valuable Player Award in 1958 and 1959 and eventually hit more home runs, 512, than any other Cub in history.*

Left: *First baseman Eddie Waitkus played for the Cubs from 1941 to 1948, then was traded to the Phillies. He has his place in Cubs history as the only ex-Cub ever to be shot by a fan. Resenting his having been traded by the Cubs to the Phillies, a Ruth Ann Steinhagen had Waitkus summoned to her room at the Edgewater Beach Hotel in Chicago on July 15, 1949, where she shot him in the chest. Waitkus was out for the season, then went on to play six more years.*

5. Times of Struggle

Perhaps in an effort to change their luck and to go back to the golden days of the franchise, the Cubs brought in the old master, Charlie Grimm, who had had a stint as a baseball announcer, to manage the club in 1960. But after a miserable 6-11 start, and with the Cubs in last place, he was fired. To replace him, Lou Boudreau, who had started broadcasting the Cub games that year, was taken out of the broadcast booth. Boudreau had had success as a manager with the Indians, the Red Sox and the Kansas City Athletics, but he couldn't do much about the Cubs.

Under Boudreau the Cubs did manage to win 54, while losing 83, finishing seventh (60-94 overall), 35 games behind the first-place Pirates. The only highlight of the season came on May 15, when Don Cardwell became the first pitcher to hurl a no-hitter in his first start after being traded by one club to another (he had been with the Phillies); Cardwell beat the Cardinals 4-0 at Wrigley Field. Not a single Cub pitcher had a winning record this year, and even Cardwell was 8-14. The other hurlers were Hobbie (16-20, leading the league in losses),

Anderson (9-11), Dick Ellsworth (7-13), Elston (8-9) and Seth Morehead (2-9). The best batter on the club was center fielder Richie Ashburn, with a .291 average. Banks, although he led the league in home runs, with 41, hit a miserable (for him) .271. Catcher Moe Thacker ended the season at .156. Boudreau was released and sent back to the microphone at the end of the season. He was to have a long and successful career as a broadcaster, although he occasionally had a problem with the pronunciation of various players' names. For example, catcher Jerry Grote (pronounced GROAT-ee) of the Mets would forever be Jerry GROAT to Boudreau.

In 1961 the Cubs tried one of the strangest and least effective managerial systems ever seen in baseball. The owner decreed that there would be a rotation of head coaches rather than a single manager. The four unfortunates were Vedie Himsl (10-21, a man who had never played in the majors), Harry Craft (7-9, a man who had played and managed before), El Tappe (42-53, who had been a Cub catcher) and Lou Klein (5-7, who had been a major league infielder). Despite all this brain power, the Cubs finished seventh that year, with an overall 64-90 record, trailing the Reds by 29 games.

The Cubs that year were not a good team. Of the pitchers, only Cardwell (15-14) and Barney Schultz (7-6) were winners. The rest looked like this: Hobbie (7-13), Ellsworth (10-11), Jack Curtis (10-13), Anderson (7-10) and Elston (6-7). Only right fielder George Altman (.303) hit over .300. Normally sure-handed third baseman Ron Santo led the league in errors, with 31. The only bright spot was that for the first time in history a Cub was named National League Rookie of the Year. He was future Hall of Fame left fielder Billy Williams. Even with all those negatives, the front office decided to continue the failed experiment of platooning the coaches, although Himsl and Craft were fired at the end of the 1961 season. Craft, at least, was able to get a job as the Houston manager in 1962.

In 1962 Charlie Metro, a former outfielder, joined Tappe and Klein as a part of a

Charlie Grimm, former manager of the Cubs, places a cap on the head of new skipper Lou Boudreau as Grimm hands over the reins on May 4, 1960. Charlie Grimm became a Cubs broadcaster on WGN later on. Lou lasted only until the end of the season, then returned to broadcasting also.

coaching triumvirate. Tappe (4-16), Klein (12-18) and Metro (43-69) directed the Cubs to a miserable 59-103, 42½ games behind the first-place San Francisco Giants. Fortunately, the Mets were now in the league, and the Cubs beat them out, since New York went 40-120. Unfortunately, since this was an expansion year, Chicago was able to finish lower than they ever had before – ninth place.

The pitching was miserable. Cal Koonce (10-10) and Barney Schultz (5-5) were the best pitchers on the staff. The hitting wasn't all that bad, with right fielder George Altman (.318), catcher Dick Bertell (.302) and left fielder Billy Williams (.298) leading the way. But two good things did happen that year. First, the platooning-of-managers plan was scrapped at the end of the season. Second, for the second year in a row, a Cub was voted National League Rookie of the Year. He was second baseman Ken Hubbs, who had played ten games in 1961.

The Cubs were finally back with a single manager in 1963. He was Bob Kennedy, who had had 16 years playing experience in the majors, and he was able to improve the teams' record to 82-80, the first time in years that the club had finished over .500. They ended in seventh place, only 17 games behind the first-place Dodgers. Dick Ellsworth, at 22-10, became the first Cub pitcher in what seemed like generations to win 20 or more games, and Lindy McDaniel had a good record of 13-7, with an amazing 22 saves. The other pitchers were Larry Jackson (14-18), Bob Buhl (11-14), Glen Hobbie (7-10) and Paul Toth (5-9). Batting was down a bit, with third baseman Ron Santo leading the team with a .297 average, followed by left fielder Billy Williams (.286). One of the highlights of the year came on May 9, when first baseman Ernie Banks set a record with 22 putouts. But tragedy struck after the season was over. Second baseman Ken Hubbs, the Rookie of the Year the previous year and a man who looked like a sure future Hall of Famer, was killed in an airplane accident near Provo, Utah, on February 15, 1964. He was 22 years old.

The Cubs slipped quite a bit in 1964, as they came in in eight place (76-86), but only 17 games behing the first-place Cardinals. It was a curious year, since the pitching was not all that bad. Indeed, Larry Jackson (24-11) led the league in wins. Buhl was 15-14 and Lew Burdette was 9-9. The losers were Dick Ellsworth (14-18), Ernie Broglio (4-7) and Lindy McDaniel (1-7), although McDaniel had 15 saves. Nor was the batting too bad, with the Cubs being led by Santo (.313) and Williams (.312). But the year was marked by one piece of stupidity when the Cubs let future Hall of Fame outfielder Lou Brock go to the Cardinals.

Nineteen sixty-five was another downer. After 56 games, and the Cubs with a 24-32 record, Kennedy was fired. (He was to re-surface in 1968 with the Oakland Athletics.) Wonder of wonders, the team brought back a member of their old troika, Lou Klein, to finish the season. It didn't help. The Cubs went 48-58 under Klein, finished at 72-90 for the season and ended in eighth place, 25 games behind the pennant-winning Dodgers. The pitching had collapsed. Only Bob Buhl, with a pathetic 13-11 record, was a winner. Bill Faul was able to break even at 6-6, as was Bob Hendley (4-4). The rest of the staff came in like this: Larry Jackson (14-21), Dick Ellsworth (14-15), Cal Koonce (7-9), Ted Abernathy (4-6, although he did have 31 saves) and Lindy McDaniel (5-6). In the batting arena, right fielder Billy Williams continued to prove that a Hall of Fame player doesn't necessarily have to play for a winner: he hit

Ron Santo became an All-Star third baseman for the Cubs during the 1960s, when Cubs fortunes turned for the better.

Above: *Lou Brock scores a run for the Cubs in 1963. In 1964 he was traded with two other players for Ernie Broglio, Bobby Shantz and Doug Clemens of the St Louis Cardinals. Brock proceeded to break lots of records, and was elected to the Hall of Fame in 1985. It was the Cubs' most infamously bad trade.*

Opposite right: *Billy Williams became the Cubs' regular right fielder in the 1960s, and went on to join the Hall of Fame after many years of success with the Cubs. He was eventually traded to Oakland.*

the best I had all year." And then, ". . . my fastball really came alive, as good a fastball as I'd had all year." In the first inning a solid fly by second baseman Glenn Beckert landed just foul in left field. In the second, Dodger center fielder Willie Davis made a great catch of a hard liner by outfielder Byron Browne that surely would have gone for extra bases. In the fifth inning the Dodgers scored a run, and Koufax was still throwing a perfect game.

With two out in the seventh inning, Koufax threw three straight balls to right fielder Billy Williams before throwing two strikes and then getting him to fly out. But Koufax's fastball was humming, and he struck out third baseman Santo, first baseman Banks and Browne in the eighth. In the ninth inning he struck out catcher Chris Krug and pinch hitter Joey Amalfitano and then faced the final batter, pinch hitter Harvey Kuenn, a .303 lifetimer who had struck out only 15 times during the season. But Koufax fanned him on three fastballs and preserved his perfect game, as the Dodgers won 1-0.

Almost forgotten was the great performance of the Cubs' left-handed pitcher, Bob Hendley, who didn't allow a run until the fifth inning, and that came on a defensive lapse following a walk, a sacrifice and a successful steal. In the seventh inning, left fielder Lou Johnson hit a bloop double, but it didn't figure in the scoring. The game ended with Hendley throwing a one-hitter. This was the only game in major-league history with just one hit.

The Cubs' front office had had enough of Klein and decided to inject a little fire into the team by hiring Leo Durocher to pilot the club in 1966. This fiery and successful manager had had a long career at the helm of the Dodgers (1939-1946, 1948) and the Giants (1948-1955). He was a fighter whose most famous quotes were, "Nice guys finish last," and "I come to play. I come to beat you. I come to kill you," and "You don't save a pitcher for tomorrow. Tomorrow it may rain."

Durocher took the Cubs to a place they had never been before – tenth place (59-103) – 36 games behind the league-leading Dodgers. Not a single pitcher had a winning record that year, although Koonce did finish with a 5-5. Ellsworth went 8-22 and led the league in losses. The rest were Holtzman (11-16), Ferguson Jenkins (6-8), Bill Hands (8-13), Hendley (4-5) and Curt Simmons (4-7). The batting was not too bad, as Santo hit .312, Beckert .287, Williams .276, Kessinger .274 and Banks .272. Still, there was no place to go but up.

And up they went in 1967. In a miraculous turn-around, they finished third (87-

.315. And third baseman Ron Santo was once again a stalwart, batting .285. But three of the regular lineup hit less than .222. They were catcher Vic Roznovsky (.221), left fielder Doug Clemens (.221) and shortstop Don Kessinger (.201). A pennant can't be won with batting like that.

The two highlights of the season were negative ones. The first one happened on May 29, when Richie Allen of the Phillies hit a Connie Mack Stadium-record 529-foot homer over the roof of the ball park off Larry Jackson of the Cubs to lead Philadelphia to a 4-2 victory. The second was even more impressive. On September 9 the future Hall of Fame Dodger pitcher, Sandy Koufax, had a record of 21-7 going into this game. Remember that the Cubs' lineup featured such slugging threats as Williams, with 34 homers and 108 RBIs that year; Santo, with 33 home runs and 101 RBIs; and Banks, with 28 roundtrippers and 108 RBIs. Koufax got through the early innings with his curve. He said it was ". . .

Above: *Glenn Beckert was the Cubs' star second baseman during their glory years in the late 1960s and early 1970s.*

Right: *Cubs manager Leo Durocher argues a call with the umpire during a game with the Mets in 1969, a year Cubs fans would like to forget.*

The next year, 1969, is not remembered with affection by Cubs fans. The league had grown to 12 teams and was divided into Eastern and Western Divisions with six teams each. The Cubs were placed in the Eastern Division, and cynics pointed out that at least the team would never finish in seventh or eighth place again. On opening day the Cubs didn't look overpowering, managing only to beat the Phillies 7-6 in extra innings, and there were rumors of trouble in the clubhouse between Durocher and virtually everybody else, including Ernie "Mr. Cub" Banks.

Nevertheless, the Cubs stayed in first place for most of the season, out-hitting and out-scoring the rest of the league. Jenkins was to go 21-15 that year, and Hands (20-14), Holtzman (17-13), Dick Selma (10-8), Regan (12-6, with 17 saves) and Ted Abernathy (4-3) were having a good year. The only losing pitcher on the staff was Nye, at 3-5. Williams (.293), Beckert (.291) and Santo (.289) were to have a fine year at the plate.

By August 13 the Cubs were still in first place, but something strange was happening to the Mets, who were nine and one-half games back. The Mets had never finished higher than ninth since they had come into the league in 1961, but Chicago fans began to worry when the Mets and Cubs had two back-to-back home-and-home series and the Cubs dropped all seven games. By September 10 the Mets had sneaked into the

74), 14 games behind the first-place Cardinals. Right-handed pitcher Ferguson Jenkins had his first 20-game year (20-13), and three other pitchers had winning records – Rich Nye (13-10), Joe Niekro (10-7) and Chuck Hartenstein (9-5, with 10 saves). The other pitchers were not really bad, either. They were Ray Culp (8-11), Bill Hands (7-8), Curt Simmons (3-7) and Bill Stoneman (2-4). Santo, as usual, led the club, with a .300 batting average and 31 homers. Behind him were Beckert (.280 and five homers), Williams (.278 and 18 homers) and Banks (.276 and 23 homers).

It was another third-place (84-78) finish in 1968, but they were only 13 games in back of the Cardinals. Jenkins (20-15) won 20 games again, and Hands (16-10), Niekro (14-10) and Phil Regan (10-5 and 25 saves) were all winners. The only losing pitchers were Ken Holtzman (11-14) and Nye (7-12). But the batting was off, as Santo hit only .246 and Banks fell to .246. Beckert led the Cubs, with .294.

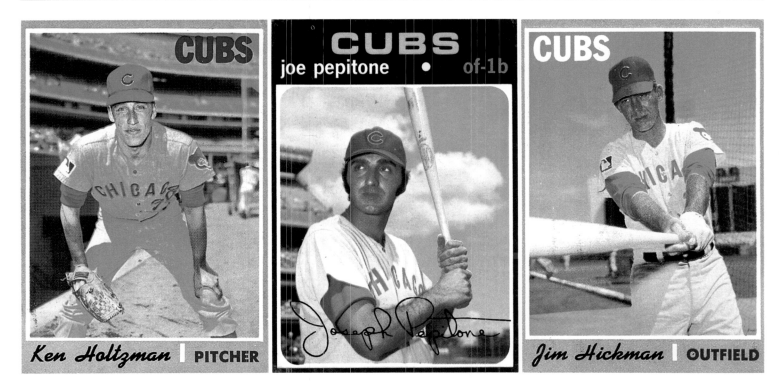

CUBS
Ken Holtzman | PITCHER

CUBS
joe pepitone • of-1b
Joseph Pepitone

CUBS
Jim Hickman | OUTFIELD

league lead. The Mets then went on to win 38 of their last 49 games, while the Cubs lost and lost. When the season ended Chicago was in second place (92-70), eight games behind the Mets, who went on to win the League Championship Series and then the World Series.

Chicago was shocked. One disgruntled fan suggested that the franchise be move to the Philippines and that the Cubs be re-named the Manila Folders. Another trau-matized Cub watcher said. "It was as if someone in my family was dying a slow death. I'd wake up each morning and say, 'They'll win today' . . . But they didn't."

Nineteen seventy was not a bad year as far as Cub history was concerned. The club finished in second place (84-78), and they were only five games behind the pennant-winning Pirates. Fergie Jenkins (22-16) had another 20-or-more-wins year. Most of the other pitchers also had a good year – Holtzman (17-11), Hands (18-15) and Milt Pappas (10-8). Only Joe Decker (2-7) and Phil Regan (5-9) had a losing season, and Regan had 12 saves. Williams (.322, with 42 homers) had one of his best years at the plate, as did first baseman Jim Hickman (.315, with 32 home runs) and Beckert (.288). But it was the beginning of the end for Ernie Banks, for he became a reserve player, hitting a lowly .252 in his 18th sea-son with the Cubs. He did, however, hit his 500th home run that year, becoming only the ninth man in history to accomplish that feat.

Nineteen seventy-one marked the end of an era – Ernie Banks retired. This great future Hall of Famer had had a great 19-year career with the Cubs, the only major league team he ever played for. Banks, "Mr.

Cub," whose favorite saying was "It's a beautiful day – let's play two," had a life-time batting average of .274 and had hit 512 home runs, 90 triples and 407 doubles out of his 2583 hits. His slugging average was .500, and he had batted in 1636 runs while scoring 1305. Truly, he was the finest player never to have had an opportunity to play in a World Series, and his was the first number to be retired by the Cubs.

Chicago finished in third place (83-79) that year, 14 games behind the first-place Pirates. Jenkins (24-13) registered his fifth straight year of winning 20 or more games, and he led the league in wins. His record was finally good enough to win him the Cy Young Award, but he seemed to be alone on the mound. Besides Jenkins, only Pappas (17-14) and Juan Pizarro (7-6) had winning records. Regan (5-5) broke even, and the others were losers – Hands (12-18) and Holtzman (9-15). The batting had im-proved, and three men hit over .300 – Beck-ert (.342), first baseman Joe Pepitone (.307) and Williams (.301).

In 1972, when the Cubs were in fourth place (46-44), Durocher was fired as man-ager. (He went on to manage Houston that same year) Whitey Lockman was brought in to replace him, and Lockman did a fine job, winning 39 and losing 26, and he took this fourth-place club into second place (85-70 and 11 games behind the Pirates). Once again Jenkins (20-12) won 20 games, Pappas went 17-7 and Rick Reuschel was 10-8. Two pitchers, Jack Aker (6-6, with 17 saves) and Tom Phoebus (3-3) broke even. The other pitchers were losers – Burt Hoo-ten (11-14), Hands (11-8) and Pizarro (4-5). At the plate, Williams was the batting champion of the league, with a .333 aver-

Above far left: *The left-hander Ken Holtzman backed up right-hander Jenkins during the late sixties, before being traded to Oakland in 1972.*

Above left: *First baseman Joe Pepitone came to the Cubs midway through 1970 and helped them finish second place in the division.*

Above: *Outfielder Jim Hickman joined the Cubs in 1968, after being a Yankee and a Dodger. He had a great offensive year in 1970, batting .322 with 42 home runs.*

age, and Santo went for .302, with right fielder Jose Cardenal finishing at .291. For his batting and his .984 fielding average, Williams was named the Major League Player of the Year by *The Sporting News*.

Lockman had no luck at all in 1973. The Cubs fell to fifth place (77-84), but they were still only five games behind the first-place Mets. The fabulous Ferguson Jenkins had a relatively terrible year, 14-16, and only Bob Locker (10-6, with 18 saves) was a winner. The rest were Hooton (14-17), Reuschel (14-15), Pappas (7-12), Aker (4-5, with 12 saves) and Bill Bonham (7-5). The hitting fell off a bit, too, with only Cardenal

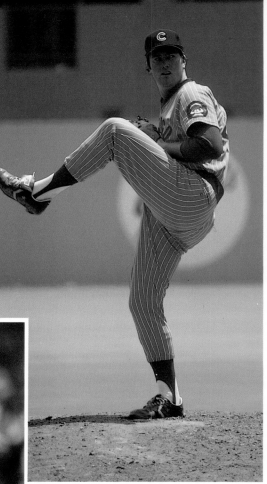

Left: *Ferguson Jenkins won 20 or more games for the Cubs six years in a row, from 1967 to 1972. His league-leading 24 wins in 1971 was enough to win him the Cy Young Award. After eight years with the Rangers and Red Sox, Jenkins achieved the 3000-strikeout mark back with the Cubs in 1982.*

Above: *Rick Reuschel was one of the Cubs' leading pitchers in the 1970s and early 1980s. Unfortunately the Cubs gave up on him, and he still is starring for the San Francisco Giants.*

Right: *Jose Cardenal slides into third base in a game against the Cincinnati Reds in 1972. Dennis Menke fails to make the play.*

(.303) hitting over .300. Then came Williams (.288), trailed by Santo and center fielder Rick Monday at .267. For some inexplicable reason, Jenkins was traded to the Texas Rangers at the end of the season for third baseman Bill Madlock and second baseman Vic Harris.

In 1974, with the club mired in fifth place (41-52), Lockman was fired and was replaced by Jim Marshall, who had played first base for a number of teams. Marshall led the club to a 25-44 record and into last place (66-96 overall), 22 games behind the first-place Pirates. The pitching, with Jenkins gone, was not very good, with only Reuschel (13-12) and Steve Stone (8-6) posting winning records. Bonham went 11-22 and led the league in losses. Rounding out the roster were Hooton (7-11), Ken Frailing (6-9), Dave LaRoche (5-6), Oscar Zamora (3-9, with ten saves) and Horacio Pina (3-4). Only Madlock (.313) hit over .300. He was followed by Monday (.294) and Cardenal (.293). Even though he was near the end of his career, it may have been a mistake when the Cubs traded Billy Williams to Oakland for pitchers Darold Knowles, Bob Locker and second baseman Manny Trillo, since, as a designated hitter for the A's, Williams drove in 81 runs the next year.

Marshall improved the standing of the Cubs in 1975, but not much. They finished fifth (75-87) and trailed the league-leading Pirates by 17½ games. The pitching improved a bit, as Ray Burris (15-10), Bonham (13-15), Stone (12-8) and Zamora (5-2, with ten saves) posted winning records. Batting was not the problem: Madlock took the National League batting title, with a .354, and Cardenal was .317. Following those two was first baseman Andre Thornton, with .293. Things were beginning to look up again.

Actually, although in 1976 the Cubs had an identical record (75-87) to the year before, they did move up to fourth place, 26 games behind Philadelphia. Reuschel (14-12), Burris (15-13), Bruce Sutter (6-3, with ten saves) and Zamora (5-3, with three saves) had winning records. And Bonham (9-13), Steve Renko (8-11), Joe Coleman (2-8, with four saves) and Knowles (5-7,

with nine saves) were not completely shabby. Madlock (.339), for the second straight year, won the league batting championship, and the next best hitter was Cardenal again (.299). But with first baseman Pete LaCock hitting .221, catcher Steve Swisher hitting .236 and the rest of the regulars not doing much better, the Cubs did not strike fear into the hearts of opposing pitchers. Marshall therefore hadn't done much, and he was fired, only to pop up managing the Athletics in 1979.

For the 1977 season Marshall was replaced by Herman Franks, who had previously managed the Giants. The Cubs had another fourth-place finish, but they at least played .500 ball, finishing at 81-81, 20 games behind first-place Philadelphia. Reuschel (20-10) finally had a 20-game season, and two other pitchers had winning years – Willie Hernandez (8-7, with four saves) and Sutter (7-3, with an amazing 31

Opposite left: *Manny Trillo was an excellent second baseman for the Chicago Cubs, and had two terms with the Cubs. Unfortunately, most of his best years were spent with other clubs in between those two terms.*

Left: *Herman Franks was the Cubs' manager in 1977, 1978, and most of 1979. He looks worried, and indeed he had plenty to worry about.*

Bobby Murcer played outfield for the Cubs in the late 1970s. He was a pretty good hitter and a pretty good broadcaster, both of which he did well for the Yankees.

saves). None of the losing pitchers had a terrible record – Burris (14-16), Bonham (10-13), Mike Krukow (8-14) and Rick's brother, Paul Reuschel (5-6). Even though Madlock was gone (traded to the Giants), as was Cardenal (traded to the Phillies), the batting held up. Left fielder Greg Gross hit .322, third baseman Steve Ontiveros hit .299 and center fielder Jerry Morales hit .290. Indeed, the Cubs had led in the early part of the season, so the year was not a complete washout.

Nineteen seventy-eight was a little better. Franks led the club to a third-place (79-83) finish, and they were only 11 games behind the first-place Phillies. They also did it without great pitching, except for fireman Bruce Sutter. Only Krukow (9-3),

Donnie Moore (9-7) and Hernandez (8-2) posted winning records. As for Sutter, even though he had an 8-10 record, he also had 27 saves. The other pitchers were disappointing – Rick Reuschel (14-15), Dennis Lamp (7-15), Burris (7-13) and Dave Roberts (6-8). First baseman Bill Buckner (.323) led the team in batting, and the next best hitters were right fielder Bobby Murcer (.281) and shortstop Ivan DeJesus (.278). The rest of the lineup was not really near them in batting average.

With the Cubs in fifth place (78-77) in 1979, Franks was fired. His interim replacement was Joey Amalfitano, who, in seven games, went 2-5. So the club ended in fifth place, with an overall 80-82 record, 18 games behind the first-place Pirates. The problem wasn't exactly the pitching. Rick Reuschel was 18-12, Lamp was 11-10 and Dick Tidrow was 11-5, with four saves. Krukow (9-9) and Sutter (6-6) broke even, and Jim McGlothen (13-14) and Holtzman (6-9) were not actually failures. Nor was the hitting all that bad. Right fielder Scot Thompson led the team, with .289, and left fielder Dave Kingman batted .288 and led the league in home runs, with 48. Following them were Ontiveros (.285), Buckner (.284) and DeJesus (.283).

The high point of the season came when Bruce Sutter, who had 37 saves, was named the Cy Young Award winner – one of the few times that a relief pitcher has been so honored. Actually, the Cubs were loaded with relievers. For example, on May 17, when the Chicagoans were beaten by the Phillies, and both pitchers took their showers in the first inning, Chicago proceeded to use five relievers, and Philadelphia four. While high-scoring games are not uncommon, particularly at Wrigley Field, what was interesting about this game was that four of the Cub relievers – Willie Hernandez, Bill Caudill, Donnie Moore and Bruce Sutter (the losing pitcher) – would go on to be considered among the best relievers of the 1980s.

Steve Ontiveros played third base for the Cubs from 1977 to 1980. His hitting was excellent, but his fielding was not. He was an inadequate replacement for Bill Madlock.

First baseman Bill Buckner was acquired from the Los Angeles Dodgers in 1977, and was a mainstay with the Cubs team until he was replaced by Leon Durham in 1984, when Buckner was traded to the Red Sox for Dennis Eckersley. Buckner is still playing as a designated hitter for Kansas City. He was a fine hitter, but will probably not be remembered as a fine fielder because of his fatal error for the Red Sox in the 1986 World Series against the Mets.

6. On the Move Again

Amalfitano, the interim manager, was gone, and Preston Gomez was brought in to begin the 1980 season. He had been the manager of both the Padres and the Astros, but he didn't last long with the Cubs. After 90 games the club stood at 38-52 and in last place, and Gomez was fired. Amalfitano was back again to finish the season. He won 26 and lost 46, and the Cubs stayed in sixth place (64-98), 27

Cub outfielder Dave Kingman could really hit home runs. He could also infuriate people and could not field very well, but he gave the Cubs some punch in the three years he played with them, including 1979, when he belted a league-leading 48 homers.

games behind the first-place Phillies. In fact, the Cubs had played like a last-place team. Only Dick Tidrow had a winning record, and that was not overwhelming – 6-5, with six saves. Of course, Sutter (5-8) turned in his usual yeomanlike job with 28 saves. Otherwise, the pitching staff was less than impressive: Reuschel (11-13), Krukow (10-15), Lamp (10-14), McGlothen (12-14), Bill Caudill (4-6), Hernandez (1-9) and Doug Capilla (2-8). Buckner led the league with a .324 batting average, but the next best regular hitter was Kingman, with .278. It was a year to forget.

Amalfitano was finally permitted to manage for a complete season in 1981, but it was a bad year to manage anywhere. This was the year of the big players' strike. In the middle of the season the ballplayers walked out and didn't come back for 50 days, the longest strike in the history of organized sports. Before the strike ended 714 games were cancelled. It was then decided that the teams who were in first place before the strike would have playoff games with the four teams who were in first place at the end of the "second season" to determine the divisional champions.

In any case, this arrangement had little to do with the Cubs, who finished sixth (15-37 and 16½ games behind Philadelphia) in the first half and fifth (21-33 and six games behind Montreal) in the second half. Of the pitchers, only Krukow (9-9) was able to break even. With more dismal records were Randy Martz (5-7), Reuschel (4-7), Tidrow (3-10, with nine saves) and Lee Smith (3-6). Since Sutter had been traded to the Cardinals during the winter, the club didn't have him to rely on as a reliever. Instead, he saved 25 games for St. Louis. The reliable Buckner led the club in hitting, with a .311, but two regulars, shortstop Ivan DeJesus (.194) and second baseman Pat Tabler (.188) batted under .200. At the end of the season, Amalfitano was gone once more.

Lee Elia was brought in to manage the Cubs in 1982, and there was some improvement. They finished fifth (73-89), 19 games behind the first-place Cardinals. Ferguson Jenkins was back, but he was in the twilight of his career (he would retire the next year) and could manage only a 14-15 record. Martz (11-10) and Tidrow (8-3) were winners, but they were hardly overwhelming. The rest of the staff posted lower marks: Doug Bird (9-14), Dickie Noles (10-13), Allen Ripley (5-7), Bill Campbell (3-6), Hernandez (4-6) and Smith (2-5). For the first time in a long while two Cubs hit over .300 – Buckner, of course (.306), and right fielder Leon Durham (.312). Shortstop Larry Bowa batted .246, but the rest of the regulars hit

over .260. No one seemed to notice, but because of the improved hitting and Lee Smith's performance as a reliever (he had 17 saves and was on his way to being a star fireman), the Cubs were on their way back. The highlight of the year happened on May 13, when the Cubs beat the Astros 5-0, to become the first team in baseball to win 8000 games.

The comeback was still not quite ready to take place in 1983. After 123 games Elia had the team in fifth place (54-69), and he was fired. Charlie Fox was brought in as interim manager, and he did a little better, winning 17 and losing 22, but the club stayed in fifth place (71-91), trailing the Phillies by 19 games. The pitching still wasn't great, with only Chuck Rainey (14-13) and Dick Ruthven (12-9) being winners.

Leon Durham came to the Cubs from the Cardinals in the trade for Bruce Sutter on December 9, 1980. He held great promise as a hitter, and became the Cubs' regular first baseman in 1984, but lost his job when Mark Grace joined the team in 1987.

But Smith, although he finished at 4-10, improved his saves number to 29, carrying an amazing 1.65 ERA. The other pitchers were Steve Trout (10-14), Jenkins (6-9), Campbell (6-8) and Noles (5-10). Right fielder Keith Moreland (.302) was the only man to hit over .300.

Then it was 1984, the miracle year that the Cub fans had been waiting for since 1945. Jim Frey, who had been the skipper of the Royals, was the new manager. The Cubs leaped out ahead early and hung on to win the National League East (96-65), six and one-half games over the Mets. Only Ruthven (6-10) and Rainey (5-7) were losers, and Rick Reuschel went 5-5 to break even. On the plus side were Trout (13-7), Dennis Eckersley (10-8), Scott Sanderson (8-5), Smith (9-7, with 33 saves), Tom Stoddard (10-6) and Rick Sutcliffe. Early in the season, Sutcliffe had been with the Indians, where he appeared in 15 games, winning four and losing five. He then came to the Cubs, and, in 20 games, he had the astonishing record of 16-1, almost single-handedly putting the team in first place.

The Cubs' bats weren't idle, either. Second baseman Ryne Sandberg hit .314, while left fielder Gary Matthews went .291, followed by first baseman Leon Durham (.279), right fielder Keith Moreland (.279) and center fielder Bob Dernier (.278). Third baseman Ron Cey had 25 homers, Durham had 23, and Sandberg had 19.

The Cubs had climbed into first place by May and doggedly held on until they won the Eastern Division championship on September 24. They then went on to face the Western champions, the Padres. Almost immediately a rhubarb started that was to have future ramifications. Wrigley Field was the only major league stadium not to have lights, and since 1971 some of the World Series games had been played at night. The Tribune Company, which now owned the club, wanted to install illumination, but Chicago fans were basically against it. The league office even went so far as to suggest that if the Cubs were to host mid-week games during the World Series, they would have to be played at

Opposite left: *Keith Moreland was a hard-hitting outfielder who also played third base and catcher. He contributed mightily to the Cubs' division championship in 1984.*

Below left: *Rick Sutcliffe was acquired by the Cubs from Cleveland in 1984 and won the Cy Young Award in that year by winning 16 games and losing only one. He remains a mainstay of the Cubs' pitching staff.*

Below: *Jim Frey managed the Cubs to the Eastern Division Championship in 1984, and is presently general manager of the team.*

Right: *Ryne Sandberg won the Most Valuable Player Award in 1984 and has been a Gold Glove at second base for the past several years in the National League.*

Opposite, top left: *Cub outfielder Gary Matthews, "The Sarge," had a miraculous year in 1984, helping to lead the Cubs to the Eastern Division title.*

Opposite, top right: *Ron Cey, a former Dodger, played third base for the 1984 Eastern Division Champions, and hit 25 homers that year.*

Opposite bottom: *Manager Jim Frey argues a call with Lee Harvey, the umpire, at Wrigley Field during the 1984 season.*

night in a neutral stadium, say Busch Stadium in St. Louis.

As it turned out, the lights weren't necessary. The first two games of the League Championship Series were played in Chicago. The Cubs overpowered San Diego 13-0 in the first game, belting out five home runs, an LCS record. They also won the second game 4-2, and then it was off to San Diego for the rest of the series. They lost all three games – 7-1, 7-5 and 6-3, and that was the end of the season. The last game was won when Durham committed an error on an easy game-ending ball hit by pinch hit-

ter Tim Flannery, which was followed by three singles. As Thomas Boswell of *The Washington Post* wrote: "When Tim Flannery's ground ball trickled into right field, knifing under Leon Durham's glove and through his Cub heart, baseball's decade of romantic good luck was finally snapped."

Still, it had been an exciting year. The whole country had enjoyed the Cubs' race while it lasted. And baseball rewarded three of the stars. With his 16-1 record and 2.69 ERA, Sutcliffe won the National League Cy Young Award. For his .314 batting average, 19 homers, 84 RBIs and .993

fielding average, Sandberg won the
National League Most Valuable Player
Award. And for his dramatic turnaround of
the Cubs, Frey was named National
League Manager of the Year.

But in 1985 Frey had a problem with his
Cubs. The team fell to fourth place (77-84),
23½ games behind the first-place Cardinals. To begin with, the pitching fell apart.
The miracle man, Sutcliffe, fell to 8-8. Ray
Fontenot (6-10), Sanderson (5-6), Ruthven
(4-7), Larry Sorensen (3-7) and George Fra-
zier (7-8) were all disappointments. Most of
the other winning pitchers were not overpowering, either. Eckersley (11-7), Trout
(9-7) and Warren Brusstar (4-3) couldn't
carry the club. Only Smith was a standout.
He won seven and lost four, while register-
ing 33 saves. The batting wasn't too
shabby, however. Moreland (.307), Sandberg (.305) and utility outfielder Thad Bosley (.328) had excellent years. Utility outfielder Davey Lopes came in at .284, and
Durham came in at .282.

In 1986, with the Cubs in fifth place (23-
33), Frey moved from the field to the front
office, becoming general manager of the
club. He was replaced by interim manager
John Vukovich, who split two games. Then
in came Gene Michael, who had been the
manager of the Yankees. He was able to
win 46 and lose 56, and the team stayed in

fifth place (70-90), 38 games behind the first-place Mets. Once again it was weak pitching that did the Cubs in. Only Ed Lynch (7-5) and Jamie Moyer (7-4) had winning records, and these would hardly put a pitcher on the All-Star team. Lee Smith, however, went 9-9 and registered 31 saves. The pitching stars – Sutcliffe (5-14), Sanderson (9-11), Trout (5-7) and Eckersley (6-11) – were impotent. Fontenot went 3-5, and Jay Baller went 2-4, with only five saves. On the batting side things fell apart, too. Sandberg led the regulars, but only with a .284 average. Following him were Cey (.273) and Moreland (.271).

In 1987, with the Cubs in fifth place (68-68), Michael was fired, to be replaced by interim Manager Frank Lucchesi. He went 8-17, and the Cubs finished the season in last place (76-85), 18½ games behind the Cardinals. Sutcliffe (18-10) finally came back to lead the league in wins, Les Lancaster (8-3) was another winner and Smith (4-10) had 36 saves. Frank DiPino (3-3) broke even. Otherwise it was not a good

Opposite left: *Manager Gene Michael meets with catcher Jodie Davis and pitcher Ray Fontenot on the mound in 1986.*

Left: *Leon Durham hit 20 or more home runs for the Cubs in 1985, 1986 and 1987.*

Below left: *Thad Bosley was a good left-handed pinch hitter during the 1984 season, and played the occasional outfield.*

Below: *Davey Lopes was acquired from the A's in 1984. Lopes was a terrific base stealer even though he was 40 years old.*

Right: *Jamie Moyer was a talented left-hander who was traded to Texas in the off-season in 1989 with Raphael Palmeiro. Since the Cubs acquired Mitch Williams, Steve Wilson, Paul Kilgus and two others in that deal, it looks good so far.*

Below: *Catcher Damon Berryhill meets on the mound with manager Don Zimmer in 1989. Berryhill looks like the Cubs' catcher for many years to come, and Zimmer did a fine job in the 1989 season.*

pitching year. Moyer (12-15), Greg Maddux (6-14), Sanderson (6-9) and Ed Lynch (2-9) rounded out the pitching roster. The hitters were more impressive. Left fielder Jerry Mumphrey led the club, with a .333 average. Behind him were Sandberg (.294), center fielder Dave Martinez (.292) and right fielder Andre Dawson (.287).

The story of the year was Dawson. He had been unhappy as a star of the Expos (1976-1986) and had declared himself a free agent. The problem was that he was making so much money that the other teams were not interested in him. So he came up with a most unusual plan. He handed the Cubs a blank check of a sort, telling the team that they could pay him what they thought he was worth. The Cubs signed him, and he took a big salary cut – signing for around a half million dollars. He had several clauses in the contract to give him bonuses based on his performance, however. And what a year he had. In addition to batting .287, he led the league in home runs, with 49, and in runs batted in, with 137, committing only four errors. He was named the National League's Most Valuable Player of the Year, despite the fact that he had played with a last-place club. Dawson got a raise the next year, of course, and at the end of the 1988 season Dawson was to sign for $2.1 million.

Brought in to manage the Cubs in 1988 was Don Zimmer. He had formerly been the skipper of the Padres, the Red Sox and the Rangers, and one of his Boston pitchers had once said that he "looked like a gerbil." Zimmer was able to manage only a fourth-place (77-85) finish, 24 games behind the first-place Mets. Still, he was a solid baseball man, and he was kept on for the 1989 season.

The story of the 1988 season was not what happened on the field, but rather what happened around it. The first major league night game had been played in Cincinnati's old Crosley Field on May 24, 1935. Over the years all the old ball parks had added lights, except for Wrigley Field. Ebbets Field in Brooklyn added lights in 1938, then it was Shibe Park in Philadelphia (1939), Municipal Stadium in Cleveland (1939), Comiskey Park in Chicago (1939), Sportsman's Park in St. Louis (1940), the Polo Grounds in New York (1940), Forbes Field in Pittsburgh (1940), Griffith Stadium in Washington (1941), Braves Field in Boston (1946), Yankee Stadium in New York (1946), Fenway Park in Boston (1947) and Briggs Stadium in Detroit (1948). The Cubs held out for almost 40 more years. Just before World War II owner Phil Wrigley had decided to install lights and had even purchased the equipment, but after the Pearl Harbor attack he donated the lights,

poles and the other paraphernalia to the war effort. As time went on Wrigley had second thoughts about the matter. His new philosophy was simple: baseball was a game of grass and sunlight. Indeed, Joe Mantegna, in his 1970s play *Bleacher Bums*, had a character utter the line, "And on the seventh day the Lord rested, and came to beautiful Wrigley Field, to watch the Chicago Cubs, play His own game, on His own green grass, under His own lights."

But now the club was owned by the Chicago Tribune Company, and the times had changed. For several years there had been attempts to install lights, but the company met a great deal of community resistance. Indeed, Wrigley had recognized that night games might disturb the tranquility of the residential neighborhood in which the park is located. Unlike most stadiums, it does not stand in isolation in a far part of the city, surrounded by huge parking lots. It is smack in the middle of a middle-class area of three-story homes separated only by streets from the walls of the ball park. Nor are they wide streets; the games behind the wall are played just a few feet from the front doors of these buildings.

Both the Chicago City Council and the Illinois State Legislature tried to pass laws forbidding the lights. A citizens' group calling itself CUBS – Citizens United for Baseball and Sunshine – was formed. They argued that the reasons given by the Tribune Company for putting in lights were not valid. Since the Cubs had drawn more than two million fans for the last two years, how would the lights let more people attend games? What about the sleep of the people across the street? What about the kids, who were always attracted to the day games? (There had long been a Chicago joke about a public announcement: "Will the lady who lost her nine children at Wrigley Field please pick them up immediately. They're beating the Cubs 10-0 in the seventh.")

Cynics pointed out that the company, which also owned the television station that broadcast Cub games, could charge higher advertising fees for a night game, and that the bedtime of a child is not a major factor in the strategic planning of professional baseball. And if the Cubs were to get into a World Series and had to have lights, portable lights could be rented. Actually, during World War II, night games had been played in Wrigley Field. They featured women's teams and played under portable lights when the Cubs were out of town.

Eventually, the lights were put in, and the first night game was scheduled to be played with the Phillies on August 8, 1988. When 13,000 tickets for the first night game went on sale June 28, beginning at 8 AM, more than 1.5 million phone calls were

Above: *Andre Dawson, though known for his prodigious hitting, is a fine right fielder and has one of the best arms in the league. Dawson came to Chicago from Montreal in 1987, the year he led the league in home runs (49) and won the MVP Award.*

Above: *The bleachers at Wrigley Field, whose fans are the most loyal of all. If the opposing team hits a home run, they throw the ball back in disgust.*

Right: *The unthinkable happened on August 8, 1988, when the lights went on for the first night game in Wrigley Field history. The gods seemed to disdain this defiance of tradition, because the rains came and the game was washed out. Wrigley was the last ball park in organized baseball to erect lights.*

placed by frenzied buyers. One man was supposed to have called 2700 times and still couldn't get through. The phone company recorded its busiest day in history. General manager Jim Frey was quoted as saying about the lights, "Would someone tell me when tradition starts? What do they want us to do, play without gloves because they didn't use them in the nineteenth century?"

On July 25 the lights were turned on in order for the Cubs to hold their first night practice. About 3000 fans paid $100 a ticket to attend the practice. The money was donated to cancer research and community projects, and the evening turned into a lawn party. The fans took the field, a rock-and-roll band played in right field and free food and beverages were passed out. In a hitting contest, Ernie Banks and Andre Dawson beat Billy Williams and Ryne Sandberg.

The lights, built by General Electric at a cost of $5 million, consisted of 26 panels on six stands overlooking the right and left sides of the field. Oddly enough, it was to cost less than $600 per game to pay for the electricity. It was also decreed that the number of night games would be held to a minimum. There would be only seven in 1988 and 18 in each following year through 2002. The light bulb had been invented three years after Chicago started playing National League baseball.

Finally the big night of illumination came. On August 8 the Cubs took the field against the Phillies. There were those who thought that God was angry with the Cubs for playing at night, for, with the Cubs leading 3-1 in the bottom of the fourth inning, a torrential downpour hit Chicago, and the game was rained out. The next night the Cubs tried again and managed to beat the Mets 6-4.

Above: *Cub shortstop Shawon Dunston scores on a wild pitch to tie the Giants at 3-3 in the fourth inning of the 1989 NLCS game three. Pitcher Jeff Brantley covers home.*

The Cubs were terrible in spring training in 1989, winning only nine games – so bad that only the kindest forecasters picked them to finish as high as fifth place. And Andre Dawson being on the disabled list for several weeks early in the season didn't help. But gradually things began to jell on this club that alternated great winning streaks with deadly losing streaks – they always came back. Two great young rookies, Jerome Walton, a center fielder, and Dwight Smith, a left fielder, began to pick up the slack, and rifle-armed Shawon Dunston, the shortstop, began to learn not to swing at bad balls. Walton, who had led the Eastern League with a .337 batting average while playing for the Cubs' AA Pittsfield farm club the previous season, and Smith, who had turned in a stellar performance for the Cubs' triple-A Iowa club in 1988, quickly became top big-league outfielders. Good seasons at the plate by Mark Grace, Walton and Ryne Sandberg, who were all among the top 11 in the league in batting average, contributed to the team's strength.

The pitching was more than adequate. Greg Maddux (19-12), Mike Bielecki (18-7), and Rick Sutcliffe (16-11) were all dependable; Mitch Williams turned in 36 saves and Les Lancaster had a strong season as well. The Cubs toyed with first place all sea-son, and on August 7 took over the lead – never to be headed. They clinched the Eastern Division championship on September 26, with four games to go, and finished the season with a record of 93 and 69 – six games ahead of the second-place Mets.

The Cubs finished strong, winning eight of their last 10 games. Then came the National League Championship Series, and an excited crowd gathered for the first night playoff game at Wrigley Field, against the San Francisco Giants. The heavy-hitting Giants quieted Chicago fans with an 11-3 win over the Cubs. In game two, however, the Cubs hammered Giant hurler Rick Reuschel for five hits and five runs, then went on to score four more in their handy 9-5 victory. It was to be their only time in the sun, however, as the series shifted to San Francisco and the Giants pro-ceeded to eke out three straight victories – 5-4, 6-4 and 3-2.

It wasn't easy to lose. Andre Dawson kept trying to go for the stands and had a miser-able time at bat, stranding a total of 19 baserunners. Les Lancaster, coming into game three to relieve Paul Assenmacher, misread the count on Robby Thompson and served up a fat fastball that the Giant hitter promptly lined over the left-field wall. After pitching brilliantly for much of game five, Mike Bielecki gave up three consecutive walks that led to a Giant win of the game and the pennant. What made the losses even more painful was the fact that the Cubs were ahead in all three games in San Francisco (4-3 in the seventh inning of the third game; 2-1 in the third inning of the fourth game; 1-0 in the eighth inning of the fifth game), and still managed to lose them all.

Despite the disappointment, there were bright spots. The Cubs' first baseman, Mark Grace, batted .647 for the series, with eight RBIs and three runs scored. His 11 hits included three doubles, a triple and a homer. Ryne Sandberg turned in an excellent performance. And Don Zimmer would later be named Manager of the Year for the National League. Detractors and even pessimistic Cub fans might point to the Cubs' NLCS blunders with the clarity and righteousness of hindsight, but the talent-laden Cubs could look forward to another promising year.

Above left: *Jerome Walton – 1989 Rookie of the Year.*

Above: *Damon Berryhill had a good '89 season, but missed the playoffs due to injury.*

Far left: *Bullpen ace Mitch Williams' 36 saves ranked him second in the league for 1989.*

Left: *Mike Bielecki helped his cause in game two of the '89 NLCS, when his first-inning single scored two runs.*

7. Odds and Ends

T he Cubs, of course, play in Wrigley Field, which seats 39,012. The stadium's home run distances in left, center and right are 355, 400 and 353 feet, and it has natural grass. Sometimes called "the most beautiful park in the majors," the friendly confines of Wrigley Field have no advertising on their ivy-covered brick walls. After every day game a flag is flown from the centerfield flagpole representing either a win or a loss, so people in the neighborhood (and on passing elevated trains) can tell how the Cubs did. The team holds spring training at Ho Ho Kam Park in Mesa, Arizona.

The Cubs, who have won more regular-season games than any other professional team in any professional sport (as of the end of the 1989 season), have become a sort of home team all over the country. Chicago superstation WGN-TV beams Cub games to cable-TV companies from a satellite, and almost every game is telecast all season.

Following a distinguished line of broadcasters – Pat Flanagan, Bert Wilson, Charlie Grimm, Lou Boudreau and Jack Brickhouse, to name a few – the voice of the Cubs now belongs to Harry Caray. Early in his career, in the late 1930s and early 1940s, Caray broadcast high school football games over radio station WCLS in Joliet, Illinois. He went to St. Louis to broadcast the Cardinals' games, spent a brief time in Oakland with the A's and then became an institution in Chicago, first with the White Sox and then with the Cubs. In 1988 Caray finished first in the enthusiasm category in a *TV Guide* sports survey, and sometimes the only highlight of a game is when he stands up in the broadcast booth in the middle of

Below: *Cub broadcaster and winner of one of the Baseball Hall of Fame's Ford C. Frick Awards in 1989 for sportscasting excellence, Harry Caray talks with manager Jim Frey at Wrigley Field in 1984. He may not be able to sing opera, but nobody sings "Take Me Out to the Ball Game" any better.*

Left: *Another Cubs broadcaster, Ronald Reagan, announced for WOC in Des Moines, Iowa, in the 1930s. He is still, of course, a Cubs fan.*

Left inset: *President Ronald Reagan helps Harry Caray do the play-by-play at Wrigley Field in late September 1988.*

Overleaf: *Wrigley Field, the home of the Cubs.*

the seventh inning and sings "Take Me Out to the Ball Game." The colorful Harry Caray has his own devoted fan following. Who knows, it's possible that in future years he may retire and be replaced by his son, Skip, who has had experience broadcasting the games of the Atlanta Hawks and Atlanta Braves.

Perhaps the most famous Cubs fan in the country is former President Ronald Reagan. A charter member of the Cubs' Die-Hard Fan Club, his first professional job was as an announcer on radio station WOC (the letters stood for World of Chiropractic) in Davenport, Iowa. The job paid $5 a week plus bus fare. He went on to become a sportscaster on WHO in Des Moines, Iowa, where he was paid $75 a week, and the job involved pretending to be broadcasting eyewitness accounts of Cub games as the plays came in over the ticker-tape.

When he got to Hollywood, and later, during his two terms as President, he still had a soft spot in his heart for the Cubs. Once, when he was to make a speech in Chicago, he actually had his helicopter pilot make a detour over Wrigley Field. In October of 1988 he was in Chicago again to make another speech and decided to go to Wrigley Field to watch a game. He ended up throwing out the first ball and doing the play-by-play on television for part of the first inning and all of the second. He later said, "You know, in a few months I'm going to be out of work, and I thought I might as well audition."

Winning or losing, that's how the Cubs affect people. Perhaps more than any other team, they are a national institution.

Cub Achievements

YEAR-BY-YEAR CUBS STANDINGS

Year	Pos.	Record	Games Behind	Manager
1876	1	52-14		Spalding
1877	5	26-33	15½	Spalding
1878	4	30-30	11	Ferguson
1879	4	46-33	11½	Anson
1880	1	67-17		Anson
1881	1	56-28		Anson
1882	1	55-29		Anson
1883	2	59-39	4	Anson
1884	4	62-50	22	Anson
1885	1	87-25		Anson
1886	1	90-34		Anson
1887	3	71-50	6½	Anson
1888	2	77-58	10	Anson
1889	3	67-25	19	Anson
1890	2	84-53	6	Anson
1891	2	82-53	3½	Anson
1892	7	70-76	30	Anson
1893	9	56-71	34	Anson
1894	8	57-75	34	Anson
1895	4	72-58	15	Anson
1896	5	71-57	18½	Anson
1897	9	59-73	34	Anson
1898	4	85-65	17½	Burns
1899	8	75-73	26½	Burns
1900	5	65-75	17½	Loftus
1901	6	53-86	37	Loftus
1902	5	68-69	37	Selee
1903	3	82-56	8	Selee
1904	2	93-60	13	Selee
1905	3	92-61	13	Selee, Chance
1906	1	116-36		Chance
1907	1	107-45		Chance
1908	1	99-55		Chance
1909	2	104-49	6	Chance
1910	1	104-50		Chance
1911	2	92-62	7½	Chance
1912	3	91-59	11½	Chance
1913	3	88-65	13½	Evers
1914	4	78-76	16½	O'Day
1915	4	73-80	17½	Bresnahan
1916	5	67-86	16½	Tinker
1917	5	74-80	28	Mitchell
1918	1	84-45		Mitchell
1919	3	75-65	21	Mitchell
1920	4	75-79	11	Mitchell
1921	7	64-89	30	Evers, Killefer
1922	5	80-74	13	Killefer
1923	4	83-71	12½	Killefer
1924	5	81-72	17	Killefer
1925	8	68-86	27½	Killefer, Maranville, Gibson
1926	4	82-72	7	McCarthy
1927	4	85-68	8½	McCarthy
1928	3	91-63	4	McCarthy
1929	1	98-54		McCarthy
1930	2	90-64	2	McCarthy, Hornsby
1931	3	84-70	17	Hornsby
1932	1	90-64		Hornsby, Grimm
1933	3	86-68	6	Grimm
1934	3	86-65	8	Grimm
1935	1	100-54		Grimm
1936	2	87-67	5	Grimm
1937	2	93-61	3	Grimm
1938	1	89-63		Grimm, Hartnett
1939	4	84-70	13	Hartnett
1940	5	75-79	25½	Hartnett
1941	6	70-84	30	Wilson
1942	6	68-86	38	Wilson
1943	5	74-79	29½	Wilson
1944	4	75-79	30	Wilson, Johnson, Grimm
1945	1	98-56		Grimm
1946	3	82-71	14½	Grimm
1947	6	69-85	25	Grimm
1948	8	64-90	27½	Grimm
1949	8	61-93	36	Grimm, Frisch
1950	7	64-89	16½	Frisch
1951	8	62-92	34½	Frisch, Cavarretta
1952	5	77-77	19½	Cavarretta
1953	7	65-89	40	Cavarretta
1954	7	64-90	33	Hack
1955	6	72-81	26	Hack
1956	8	60-94	33	Hack
1957	7	62-92	33	Scheffing
1958	5	72-82	20	Scheffing
1959	5	74-80	13	Scheffing
1960	7	69-94	35	Grimm, Boudreau
1961	7	64-90	29	Himsl, Craft, Tappe, Klein
1962	9	59-103	42½	Tappe, Klein, Metro
1963	7	82-80	17	Kennedy
1964	8	76-86	17	Kennedy
1965	8	72-90	25	Kennedy, Klein
1966	10	59-103	36	Durocher
1967	3	87-74	14	Durocher
1968	3	84-78	13	Durocher
1969	2	92-70	8	Durocher
1970	2	84-78	5	Durocher
1971	3	83-79	14	Durocher
1972	2	85-70	11	Durocher, Lockman
1973	5	77-84	5	Lockman
1974	6	66-96	22	Lockman, Marshall
1975	5	75-87	17½	Marshall
1976	4	75-87	26	Marshall
1977	4	81-81	20	Franks
1978	3	79-83	11	Franks
1979	5	80-82	18	Franks, Amalfitano
1980	6	64-98	27	Gomez, Amalfitano
1981	6	38-65	11½	Amalfitano
1982	5	73-89	19	Elia
1983	5	71-91	19	Elia, Fox
1984	1	96-65		Frey
1985	4	77-84	23½	Frey
1986	5	70-90	38	Frey, Vukovich, Michael
1987	6	76-85	18½	Michael, Lucchesi
1988	4	77-85	24	Zimmer
1989	1	93-69		Zimmer

CUBS POST-SEASON RECORD

World Series

The Cubs won the pennant six times before the beginning of the World Series – 1876, 1880, 1881, 1882, 1885 and 1886.

Year	Opponent	Win-Loss
1906	White Sox	2-4
1907	Tigers	4-0, 1 tie
1908	Tigers	4-1
1910	Athletics	1-4
1918	Red Sox	2-4
1929	Athletics	1-4
1932	Yankees	0-4
1935	Tigers	2-4
1938	Yankees	0-4
1945	Tigers	3-4

Playoffs

Year	Opponent	Win-Loss
1984	Padres	2-3
1989	Giants	1-4

HALL OF FAMERS

Name	Position	Year Elected
Grover Cleveland Alexander	pitcher	1938
Adrian "Cap" Anson	outfield, manager	1939
Ernie Banks	first base, shortstop	1977
Lou Boudreau	manager	1970
Roger Bresnahan	catcher, manager	1945
Lou Brock	outfield	1985
Three Finger Brown	pitcher	1949
Frank Chance	first base, manager	1946
John Clarkson	pitcher	1963
Kiki Cuyler	outfield	1968
Dizzy Dean	pitcher	1953
Johnny Evers	second base, manager	1946
Jimmie Foxx	first base	1951
Frankie Frisch	manager	1947
Burleigh Grimes	pitcher	1964
Gabby Hartnett	catcher, manager	1955
Billy Herman	second base	1975
Rogers Hornsby	shortstop, manager	1942
Monte Irvin	outfield	1973
Highpockets Kelly	first base	1973
King Kelly	outfield, catcher	1945
Ralph Kiner	outfield	1975
Chuck Klein	outfield	1980
Freddie Lindstrom	third base, outfield	1976
Rabbit Maranville	shortstop	1954
Joe McCarthy	manager	1957
Robin Roberts	pitcher	1976
Al Spalding	pitcher, manager	1939
Joe Tinker	shortstop, manager	1946
Rube Waddell	pitcher	1946
Hoyt Wilhelm	pitcher	1985
Billy Williams	outfield	1987
Hack Wilson	outfield	1979

ALL-TIME CUB CAREER BATTING LEADERS

Games Played	Ernie Banks	2528
At Bats	Ernie Banks	9421
Hits	Cap Anson	3041
Batting Average	Riggs Stephenson	.336
Home Runs	Ernie Banks	512
Runs Scored	Cap Anson	1719
Runs Batted In	Cap Anson	1715
Strikeouts	Ron Santo	1271
Stolen Bases	Frank Chance	404

ALL-TIME CUB CAREER PITCHING LEADERS

Innings Pitched	Charlie Root	3131
Wins	Charlie Root	201
Losses	Charlie Root	156
Winning Percentage	Three Finger Brown	.649
Earned Run Average	Three Finger Brown	1.80
Strikeouts	Ferguson Jenkins	2038
Game Appearances	Charlie Root	605
Shutouts	Three Finger Brown	50
No-Hitters	Ken Holtzman	2
Saves	Lee Smith	180

SINGLE-SEASON CUB BATTING RECORDS

Batting Average	Rogers Hornsby	.380	1929
Hits	Rogers Hornsby	229	1929
Home Runs	Hack Wilson	56	1930
Runs Batted In	Hack Wilson	190	1930
Game-Winning RBIs	Gary Matthews	19	1984
Singles	Earl Adams	165	1927
Doubles	Billy Herman	57	1935, 1936
Triples	Frank Schulte	21	1911
	Vic Saier	21	1913
Slugging Percentage	Hack Wilson	.723	1930
Strikeouts	Byron Browne	143	1966
Hitting Streak	Ron Santo	28	1966
Grand Slam Home Runs	Ernie Banks	5	1955

SINGLE-SEASON CUB PITCHING RECORDS

Wins	Three Finger Brown	29	1908
Losses	Dick Ellsworth	22	1966
	Bill Bonham	22	1974
ERA	Three Finger Brown	1.04	1906
Winning Percentage	Rick Sutcliffe	.941	1984
Strikeouts	Ferguson Jenkins	274	1970
Saves	Bruce Sutter	37	1979
Innings Pitched	Grover Alexander	363	1920
Game Appearances	Ted Abernathy	84	1980
	Dick Tidrow	84	1980
Shutouts	Three Finger Brown	10	1906